Among the Hills
of Ardnaree

ORLA
KELLY
PUBLISHING

Nora Feehan

978-1-914225-66-6

Orla Kelly Publishing
Kilbrody,
Mount Oval,
Rochestown,
Cork,
Ireland

J.F. Daly
The Crescent
1909-1996

I'd like to acknowledge the help I have received from several people throughout this book's long journey. Firstly, I wish to thank Orla Kelly for her patience and expertise in bringing this project to fruition; to Ronan Colgan, whom I first approached about the idea and gave me firm belief in what I was setting out to do, and to Kersten Mierken for editing. I'd also like to thank my family, my sisters Mary & Ursula, my brother Terry and nephew Richard McElwee - for their unwavering support throughout this process. I'd especially like to acknowledge Mary for her wisdom and guidance. I cherished her memories of the late Nora Feehan. Finally, I wish to remember my late parents Rosamond and Jodie Daly for it was they who carefully kept the original notebooks in safe storage and allowed a time gone by to live on.

Oliver

Contents

Remembering Nora, whose wonderful stories and poems have finally been published.

(1876-1956)

About the Author

Nora Feehan was born in Tyrrellspass on 26 Nov 1876 to an American mother, Mary Anne or Anne Marie Rickard (1836-1902). Mary Anne married Francis Feehan, (Grocer and Publican) in Rochfortbridge in 1858. He died in 1881 aged 46. It's interesting that Nora frequently wrote under the nom de plume of her father 'Francis O'Fiachran'. Nora was the youngest one of ten children with only four surviving into adulthood. She had two brothers and seven sisters. None of the girls ever married.

Nora as a young lady

Nora taught in the local National School in the 1900's and is pictured below with her class in 1910 and again in 1914 with fellow teachers. She died in 1956.

Tyrrellspass National School 1910 with Nora Feehan standing to the left

Norah Feehan pictured seated with fellow teachers 1914

During her life time she took a great interest in Irish History and local folklore. She contributed many articles of local interest to the 'Westmeath Examiner' in the 1930's. Over a period of 70 years, she penned on old school notebooks a series of short stories. These had remained hidden away until their recent discovery.

Feehan's tales, told with some wonderful turn of phrases from the time, are charming in many ways and bring the reader through the simple lives of people from rural Ireland in the late 1800's and early 1900's.

Nora circa 1953

Prologue

Over 90 years ago Nora Feehan, a writer/teacher/artist in Tyrrellpass, Co Westmeath penned a series of short stories that have remained hidden away until their recent discovery. She died in the early 1950's.

The short stories were written in the early 1900's. At least two of the stories refer to life in Ireland in the 1870's/1880's. She frequently used her father's name Francis O'Fiachran - I assume to try and get her work published.

Oliver

November 2021

Among the Hills of Ardnaree

A tale from the 1870s

By Francis O'Fiachran

(Nora Feehan)

Kind, kind and gentle is she,
Kind is my Mary,
The tender blossom on the tree
Cannot compare wi' Mary
Gabriel H. Barbour

1

It was a red letter day in Mary McLaughlin's life, this, and there was joy in her bright young face and sunshine in the dark brown depths of her eyes as she tripped along the moss-grown pathway, under the big trees of the wood; for Mary had an inveterate dislike of roads, seeing that they generally led in the long or short to towns; but in here amongst the giants and the dwarves of plant life, she was in her glory. Not a glimpse of the white highway, with its shifting grey shadows of branches, could obtrude itself through the crumbling wall to detract from the primeval loveliness of the scene. And surely since the far-off days when her ancestors, the great McLaughlins, had caused these gnarled old beeches and chestnuts to be planted, no brighter little figure had honoured them by preferring their shade to all besides.

Her face was a characteristic one. About the red lips, closed so softly yet firmly, there were curves that told of a determined will, when Mary cared to use it; while in the proud arch of the black eyebrows, and the lines of the aquiline nose a physiognomist would have discovered traces of the old fighting spirit that had caused the McLaughlins of past generations to be regarded with dread by the English of the Pale. But there was beauty as well as character in Mary McLaughlin's face, with its delicate pink-white tints, incised in a framing of shining auburn tresses; and there was a certain whimsical trick in it, too; for on the heels of the determined look could follow such a sparkling, mischievous smile as would fain make the beholders join, out of pure sympathy.

The smile of today had more of happiness than of mischief, as she looked up through the green branches at the glorious spring morning sky, and down at the blue and white violets dotting the green carpet of the wood.

'Oh, dear flowers and trees!' she exclaimed. 'My own dear friends! Only think, I am going to the old farmhouse at last. I am really going there to sew at the window under the big hill, where the wallflowers are always dancing, and nodding in time. And I can stop on Sundays too. How pleasant it will all be; and what wonderful excursions I will make along the backs of the stream. And here's the gap in the wall. Why, I declare, I'm nearly there already. I was so joyful I didn't feel the time passing.' And Mary jumped lightly over the loose stones and came crashing against a tall man who was passing just then.

'Oh, Mary, is it you? Out so early in the morning.'

It was the master of the farmhouse – a distant cousin of Mary's into the bargain – who spoke.

'I beg your pardon,' said Mary, somewhat confused. 'I didn't think there was anyone coming, or I would not have gone so quickly,' and she gave half a shy look at him; for if there was any one person Mary stood somewhat in awe of, it was this big, square-shouldered kinsman, who was always so full of his farms, horses, cattle and tillage, that if it hadn't been for the collision, very likely he would never have noticed her. The truth was, she knew very little about him, except that he was, as people had it, a Protestant; able to remain staunch, in spite of all his Catholic mother and sister could do to alter his belief. And this gave her a somewhat distorted notion of him. As oftentimes the shallow noisy brook attracts more notice than the deep, smooth-flowing river, beneath whose wave the golden ore may be concealed, so Charlie Stuart's manner – among those with whom he was not well acquainted – suggested pride, and even moroseness. In reality, only the truest, kindly and sensitive nature, partly concealed beneath the shadow of a somewhat shy and distant manner, existed.

There was no doubt, however, of his obstinacy where religion was concerned, and this was perhaps the main source from which the popular opinion concerning him sprang.

'I hope your father is trying to mind his business. Is James Maloney with you still? I'm thinking it would be much better for your father if the same James were in some other sphere.'

Mary's face grew pale and flushed in turns; and the proud little head was raised a bit higher in the air, and again it was lowered, and the dark eyes fixed on the ground, to prevent him from seeing the tears of wounded pride rising there.

What right had he to go criticising her father? Why did everyone remind her that her father was not as he should be?

'Don't fret; he'll be improving now, when he has you grown up, to help him, Mary,' and Charlie looked at her with something like pity in his eyes.

'I believe you're going down to give the mother a helping hand at the sewing. They'll be wanting to knock too much out of you now, but don't kill yourself for them, child'.

And turning away he left her, half angry, and again half pleased, at being, for the first time, the object of his notice.

'I wonder he knew may name,' she said, but perhaps Charlie, with all his distant ways, could know as much as another when he chose.

Many years before, another Mary McLaughlin, a cousin of our heroine's father, had taken it into her head to run away with and get married to Harry

Stuart. When her family – who were very well-to-do at the time, in spite of frequent confiscations – discovered the disgrace under which they were brought, by being allied, whether they would or not, to the hated English Protestants of the Pale, a ban had gone forth from a meeting of the clan that there should be no further communication with her.

And this former Mary was as proud and as independent, in her own way, as the proudest in her clan; so she never offered to be the first to hold out the olive branch. Only once had she humbled herself, and it was when, on the night of her marriage, she had boldly entered her father's house and insisted on being given an old picture that had hung over her head from childhood. She did not ask for the chests of linen she had spent so many hours spinning, or for the fortune she had so diligently earned. No! All she wished not to leave behind was the old mildewed picture.

And her father had sent it out to her in the hands of a servant; and when her mother, losing all her anger and pride, had made as if she would take the strayed sheep back to her heart, the father had stepped before her and had said that, for such a disgrace as the family had suffered by Mary's conduct, there was no forgiveness.

So Mary had gone away in the dark night, down the lonely woodland road to the home and the husband she had chosen. And it was a beautiful home, the old cottage among the woods, and Harry Stuart was a kind and loving husband; and many fair children had grown up around them.

But a shadow ever rested on Mary's heart, for her husband, kind and lenient in every other way, had an inherited, unreasoning bigotry where his religion was concerned; and it was a punishment as heavy as her family could wish when, on a Sunday morning, she had to witness her fine boy and her five lovely girls turn with their father towards the Protestant church while she walked all alone to mass, there to be treated to the pitying glances of her neighbours.

But the odd picture still hung over her bed, and many an hour had she knelt before it, praying God to forgive the headstrong ways of her youth; and to teach her husband what she had not the power to teach.

And when he was away at fair or market, the children would be gathered around her while she explained to them, as well as she could, the truths of religion.

But the schools for young Catholics in her day were few and far between; and her parents, being more or less worldly, had not troubled to go very deep into theology with her; so she had little else than the old trusting faith to help her.

It would have been touch and go with Mary, had not her spirit of prayer conquered all difficulties; and, one by one, she saw her five girls turn to the practice of her own religion, but not while they dwelt in the old home; for their father remained as staunch as ever, and her son Charlie was his double in every way.

From the minute the lad was able to go to a fair he was his father's shadow and Mary Stuart boasted: let the girls do as they could, Charlie was able to keep the True Blue Flag flying.

As time wore on, Harry Stuart arrived at the day when he was no longer able to visit his beloved fields and one evening he called his little grandchild to help him to the stile, 'till he could see the men cut the hay in the river meadow for the last time.

'Maria,' he said, 'call up your father to me.'

And when honest Joe Wyer − his daughter's husband − had come, the old man, stretching out his hand to him, said, 'Joe, you know the way I want to die.'

And Joe, his eyes glistening with tears of joy and sorrow, had led the old man in and soon, mounting the grey nag, was speeding away to the village for Father John.

And who could paint the feelings of Mary Stuart, as she knelt before the old picture to pray for her husband, who had come to the vineyard at the last; or who, again, could tell the tranquillity and peace of the old master, as he lay expecting the summons; and with but one thing to trouble him, and that the matter on which he had prided himself for years – namely the son who was to keep the True Blue Flag flying over the homestead. But above all, who could describe the anger of Charlie, when he heard that his father, who had been so careful in training him to his own religion, had now, as he said, become a renegade to it.

'Charlie,' said the old man, 'you see that picture there, that your mother has prayed before, for me, since the night long ago that she brought it here as her only dowry. Didn't I often teach you to sneer at it, my boy, and to believe that it was a sort of household idol, the sole object of your mother's misguided belief? Well, I've been looking into it this while back, and the words under it have been ringing in my old brain. Read them for me, Charlie.'

And Charlie had complied and had read the words, in a voice with a tone of contempt that had also a breath of grief in it. 'Behold I stand at the door and knock. If any man shall hear my voice, and open to me the door, I will come in and sup with him, and he with me.'

'Ah yes, said old Harry, 'yes! The knocking has been going on in my heart a long time now; and I was slow to hear and perhaps too proud to yield; and I hope God will forgive me for coming so late. Your mother could not explain matters so well to me, but I have been reading things up, and Father John has put my last doubts to rest. Speak to him, Charlie, I would like to see you as I am now, before I go.'

And Charlie had held his head high and had spoken as became his early education. 'Father! I will be no renegade if you are. I will hold to the religion of my ancestors and will have nothing to say to such superstition as that.'

And the old man, stretching out his hand to his wife, had said, 'Pray for the boy, Mary, and he will think like me in the end.'

So the years had passed, and Mrs Stuart had continued to pray, but apparently without any result; for there was no more regular attendant at church services than Charlie.

2

But gone is all their power – the very spot
Where many a time they triumphed, is forgot.

But what of the McLaughlins? How had they fared all this time? Well, like many another family that had owned broad acres of the country from time immemorial, they gradually lost their grip and by degrees left their native land for another sphere of action.

And when John McLaughlin was at last refused a renewal of his lease, and the remnant of his ancestral inheritance was seized by a greedy landlord, and he and his young daughter Mary – with an account of whom this story opens – set sail for Australia, it could be said that Ardnaree had witnessed the departure of the last of the old name.

But John McLaughlin, soured as he had been by the loss of his fine land and the levelling of his old home, could not settle down contentedly anywhere and one fine morning, a few years later, had returned to his native place accompanied by a person who had once been a yard boy to the McLaughlins and who, emigrating to the colonies, had made a large fortune, which fact he was anxious to advertise.

This was James Maloney, of whom we have heard Charlie Stuart speak. He was a middle-sized man with, perhaps, rather more of a body than was good for his legs. His face was red, his eyes were red and any fragments of hair on his head or face that weren't a dirty grey were red also.

From knuckle to tip his bony fingers were encased in every variety of silver and gold rings, while across the front of his ample waistcoat − which was seldom without two or three buttons open (to give him room to swell, as Charlie Stuart used to say) − hung a heavy gold chain with so many ornaments hanging from it as would set up a jeweller. It may better describe his love of ornamentation and show to say that the first name given him by the rising generation of Ardnaree and neighbourhood, was 'the Fellow with the Cuthriments.'

Such was James Maloney, an extensive man, both in the matter of dress, in the matter of flesh and bone, and with regard to the inner qualities, in the matter of villainy. John McLaughlin had bought a few acres and a house on the borders of Ardnaree bog; and if he had worked as his daughter did there is no doubt he would have managed to live in fairly comfortable circumstances; but pride held sway in his heart, a strange pride, which made his shrink from driving the few head of cattle raised on his bit of land to fair or market.

'Many a day,' he would exclaim, 'my father's cattle shook the road, going to Ballinasloe or Athlone; how could I face the country, with a couple of punkawns of calves?'

But strange are the ways of the luckless: while he held this notion with regard to himself, he never once troubled about what his daughter did. She might escort lame Paddy to the fair, with the punkawns, if she would. And she would, and she did. And she never thought what the people might say when, as things grew worse, she hoisted her churn of buttermilk on the asses' cart and, driving into town, sold in pints and quarts, or carried her bucket of fowl to the market. And what did people say? Why, that there wasn't a nicer-mannered girl, or a better manager in the country, if that lazy, mean old father of hers only gave her a fair chance.

But he didn't give her a chance, and his sorrows must be drowned in drinking the recompense of her labour, and gambling what little remained, with Maloney, and a few more choice spirits.

Well did Mary know that Maloney was the evil genius; that his strongest and best efforts were being used to get them into his power and to render her father more hopeless every day. But worst of all, well did she know his reason for all this; his reason for following him from Australia. Yes! It was all caused, by his desire to make her, Mary, his wife, in spite of herself, in spite of fate. Had he not told her so?

And Mary shrank from his look, as she never shrank from anything before.

Often when she passed the old farm of the Stuarts, going to Mass, she longed to be able to visit those kinsfolk of hers. All looked so calm and peaceful there. Was it that, deep in her heart, she knew the tall, broad-shouldered master, with his obstinate, dark ways, would have it in him to kick such a one as James Maloney into the lough below the crossroads?

Well, her longing was to be gratified today. Mary had taken to sewing lately, since even the punkawns had disappeared; and to her surprise and joy, one evening a boy from the old farm had come with a letter from the mistress, asking her to give a helping hand at some quilting and other things. So on this beautiful spring morning, Mary

'Here are four quilts I patched myself in the winter nights and I never got time to quilt them yet; so between us, we'll do great work now. I'm thinking we'll keep Eliza busy making tea for us.'

Thus the old mistress bustled around and chatted and made her younger helper feel at home. And soon the tea and the hot cake were dispatched, and they were in full swing at the work. Oh, what a pleasure it was to Mary, to sit at the window where the wallflowers danced, and in the intervals of work, to look out at the busy farmyard, and to listen to the merry, indescribable buzz of the bleating of the lambs, and the deep bass lowing of the calves — and the unmusical musical shuffle of the pigs; and the droll singing chuckle of the hens as they turned in various directions, with such a bustling business-like air as to make one feel surprised when their peregrinations ended in nothing better than shuffling out their feathers and falling sideways in the straw barn door, with one eye thrown up enquiringly at the weather, and their legs stuck out so straight that it seemed they could never bend again. And how pleasant it was, in the falling shades of evening, when the last brewing of tea was over, to cross the haggart stile into the wood.

And how joyful Mary felt when, on the hilltop, she paused to look back at the pleasant old place, and to think that the following night, when she had given old Anne Smullin directions for what to do in her absence from home, she would sleep down there, among the whispering woods. Then these thoughts were laid aside for others more exciting. What was the meaning of the commotion down the hillside, and this noise of bursting brambles, and bushes pushed aside by some large body?

Mary had turned and was fleeing in terror of a prospective mad dog, when a voice with a touch of humour in it called after her, and Mary recognised it as the voice of Charlie, who had not returned from the tillage when she left the farmhouse.

'What did you run away for, so suddenly?' he said. 'Don't you know I'll be wanting jobs done as well as the mother? Here, Mary, have you still enough left after the day to mend this for me?' And he held up his arm, showing a great break in the sleeve, where it had caught in the machinery of the plough. 'I thought I would be home before you left,' he said, 'as the mother's sight is getting bad at night, and you might as well turn out the house altogether, as to ask Eliza to put in a stitch. And it's my only working coat.'

Mary, in a good-humoured way, took out the needle fastened so carefully in her jacket and soon her busy fingers were employed in repairing the tattered sleeve as quickly as possible. And the tall farmer said nothing at the time but let his dark-grey eyes rest half-humorously now on the busy fingers, and now on the determined, proud little face of their owner. 'I wonder will you be able to repair a broken heart as handy as that?'

Mary looked into his eyes with not a trace of embarrassment − for why should she feel embarrassed, reader? Wasn't he nearly old enough to be her father in the first place − she had heard that he was coming up on forty. And in the second, wasn't he a Protestant? And in the third, wasn't he a distant cousin?

So Mary answered quite off-hand that she didn't think she would ever have the honour of repairing any broken heart.

'And why not, Mary? Do you think it likely you will get through life without inflicting a wound in someone's heart?'

Mary thought of James Maloney. Was this what he meant? 'Don't be talking such nonsense,' she said, half crossly, 'no one will get their hearts wounded, they will be safe enough. I never want to do any such thing. I have made up my mind to live and die a comfortable old maid. So finish up now and go home, and don't be tormenting me'.

And she flew away down the road path, leaving him to gaze after her with a half-humorous light still in his eyes. And it hadn't left them when he vaulted across the stile into the haggart.

3

His homely garb has not fashion's graces
But it wraps a frame that is lithe and strong
His brave hand may show labour's traces.
But 'tis honest toll that does no man wrong.
J.D. Sullivan

So the days passed at the farm and each had a new pleasure for Mary, as they glided away all too quickly. She was beginning to be as much at home there now as she was in her own home. Her love for the old place and its old mistress was steadily on the increase and between herself and its master, a strange friendship had sprung up. Could this be called friendship? Mary had lost her awe of him entirely now, for she began to see that, in spite of his outside manner, he could be as humorous as the best of them amongst his intimates and no one loved a droll story more than he, or could come around the old men for the purpose of getting them to tell one better.

Sometimes he would be coming up the hill of a morning and would meet her on the top and it was his greatest pleasure to stop and draw her out on some subject he knew they differed on. And the stronger the opposition on Mary's part, the more provoking he would become, and the more he would smile when she flitted off indignantly down the hill.

And after, all nothing pleased her better than to start off to the field he was working in with some of his favourite beverage, tea; even though she generally returned from these expeditions somewhat the worse off after an argument.

In fact, those farm hands who aired golden opinions − especially the old Nanny Neill, who could seldom be pleased in a girl − said that Mary always reminded her of the dove from the Ark, who could find no rest for the sole of her foot.

And oh, the difference between those nights and the other nights she had known at home, when James Maloney ogled her over his glasses of stout. Those nights when work would cease and the yard boys would have a come-all-ye around the fire, before starting to switch. And Mary would join in and give them many an old ballad she had learned from the Irish exiles who used to visit her father's hut in the Australian bush.

On these occasions the master would stretch himself on the bench in the corner, his eyes half-closed and his favourite dog leaning up against him – without joining either in the come-all-ye or cards, or whatever was going forward.

But there isn't a doubt that, from under those half-closed eyelids, many a stolen glance wandered to the bright little face of Mary; and her joyous laugh threw a more contented look over his face. However, this kind of peace seldom lasted the night through for him, for Mary in her working hours had heard many a tale from his mother on his obstinacy where religion was concerned, and as she had read a lot, and had very clear reasons for this faith that was in her, she grew ambitious of converting this misguided kinsman.

Sometimes the question would be raised on the Four Marks of the Church and as, one by one, Mary proved to Charlie that he possessed some of them, he would quote Bible passages and talk about religion having gone wrong. And Mary would say: 'How?' and 'When?'

And Charlie would say, 'I know it has,' and Mary would say, 'Prove it.'

And so the fight would go on, now on one point, now on another; and still Mary would have the last word – aye the victory, too. And Mrs Stuart would sit – her knitting held at a standstill, while she looked over it, now at Mary, with a nod and a smile of approbation; and then again at her son, with a dissenting shake of the head.

And Charlie would end up frowning heavily at Mary and telling her he hated to hear a person talking that had no depth in them. And Mary would have the last word again, till one night it grew so strong that, seizing her hat, and declaring that she would not remain under the same roof another instant with such a man, she dashed into the rain and darkness and was only prevented from starting off through the wood, in spite of the ghosts of high and low degree to be seen disporting themselves there in the dim light, by the obstreperous man himself seizing her, by sheer force, and depositing her safe and sound in his own special nook by the fire; at the same time declaring that she had depth in her, that she was as deep as the well in Ardnaree bog, that even the sappers and sinners wouldn't fathom.

And it wasn't five minutes before they were back on the old subject again.

'You are the most provoking man I ever met! Will nothing convince you? Don't you see you are all in opposition to each other? How else could it be when you have no head?'

'Suppose now you had no head, yourself, and that your arms had an inclination to go one way, and one of your feet one side and the other another side, what way would you be?'

'Begorra, I'm thinking,' said Jimmy O'Farrell – the occasional and privileged beggar man – 'I'm thinking he'll be the mortal picture of ould Birdie Rachard that had one foot making for Croghan Hill, and the other for Knockastia.'

And the argument dissolved in a laugh, with a slight shaft from Mary of, 'God help the woman that'll get you,' and another shaft in return: 'We'll be all on a level in that line, I'd like to be listening at the keyhole after the first week.'

Then Mary, suddenly becoming serious, would remark, 'Do you believe, Jim, in people who cannot agree marrying each other?'

'Begorra I do, miss. I think they often have a stronger regard for one another than them quiet craythers. I used to stop at a house one time, and they be always having a friendly tiff like that; an' be the morthial! When herself died, he wasn't any time about followin' her, glory be to God! An' he told me himself it was the loss o' the argumentation was complainin' him.'

'Well, what have you to say to that, Mary?' and a droll look lay in Charlie's dark eyes.

'All I have to say is this – that there's no love lost between me and you, anyway.'

And Charlie would say, 'No, not as much as would satisfy the hunger of a midge.'

'I doubt if what you are after sayin' is true, Jimmy,' said Mary. 'I felt it in myself, that if I really cared for any man, I'd find his ways always agree with mine.'

'Even if he were an unbeliever?' put in Charlie, for which he was rewarded with a look of scorn.

'At least I never would think of marrying any man unless I felt so towards him. What do you say, Mrs Stuart?'

'Well, I partly agree with Jimmy. I don't think it's the ones that pass the quietest through life can care the most. Those easy-going people are was standing inside the gate of the cottage for the first time.

'Well, Mary, you are an early bird,' said Mrs Stuart, coming out and bringing her, the hand, into the old-fashioned parlour with its grandfather clock ticking solemnly in the corner and its mirror of a hundred years of age, perhaps, in which one's face seemed to widen to an enormous extent; and its glass case of old china and the thousand and one strange ornaments that accumulate, in the course of years, in an ancient parlour.

'Let me take your bonnet for you, dear. You must feel very lonely away there in the bog, by yourself. Now that the ice is broken, you will often come over a while. You won't eat idle bread with me, either.' And Mrs Stuart, with a smile in the brown eyes that were so like Mary's own, stooped and kissed the fair brow through the tossed auburn hair – and love of the mother she barely remembered came over Mary at the kind words and the soft caress.

'Eliza, get ready a cup of tea for Mary and me, and make a hot cake, just a small one for ourselves, before we begin work. It will help us on. I know you're fond of tea, Mary, where was there ever a McLaughlin that wasn't?'

still the same in the way of affection. They haven't the power to care like hot-headed people. I think the love that lasts the longest is that in which one and the other can give and take and forgive'

'Now, Mary'.

4

Soon, and to Mary's disappointment, it must be said, the work was finished and she was standing one evening at her own door in the failing twilight, looking away towards the distant woods with the mist drifting across them on the wings of the wind and wondering what they were doing at the farm. And was Jimmy gone yet, and was Charlie glad she wasn't there to torment him about religion?

And then she fell to thinking about the wife he was soon to bring home to the old farm; and would she argue with him? And in her heart she envied her; not, as she said, for the sake of the man she was getting, but for the sake of her dear old place, in which she would live and die.

And then Mary fell to dreaming about the cherished ideal. And while she buried herself getting supper ready for her father, a strange feeling of dissatisfaction and depression stole over her which almost made her nervous; for she did not understand that it was simply lonely she felt.

Soon, John McLaughlin arrived accompanied by Maloney and another crony. 'By gosh,' said Maloney, stretching himself on the settle bed, 'he's a lucky blaggard, is Charlie Stuart. As I was just saying, she owns Ardnasheelin – not speaking at all about the big fortune in cash she'll get, and sure there's only a double ditch between that farm and his own.'

'What a nuisance this love is, Mack. By this and by that! I think we're very soft people here, so I do.' And Maloney's eyes were fixed on Mary. 'For instance, look at a man like me, throwing myself away here, and all through this softness of mine, when I could get as good a match, and better than Stuart, any day.'

'It's the fellows like him, who don't yield to their feelings, that go ahead in the world, so it is. But talking of feeling, what business have I, putting feelings and the name of Stuart in the same breath. The hardened vagabond that cased his old father going out of this world because he ventured to assert himself at the last.'

'Do 'ye think will he turn with her?' asked the crony. 'Turn! Oh, the devil a turn, ever he'll turn.'

'Aye! But they say she doesn't mind much herself; all she wants is the boy.'

'I believe so, and, upon my conscience! She' making a dashed fool of herself. The deeper you go with that fellow, the darker he is – here, hand me that bottle of stout off the dresser, Mary – there's no knowing him – why don't you do what you're bid, girl? Mack! You'll have to chastise this girl of yours soon, I'm afraid. I suppose evil communication corrupts good manners; she's been in a certain place more than good for her this while back.'

'If you want drink, Mr Maloney, you can hire a servant for the purpose of handing it to you; and as for your insinuations about my cousin, they are nothing more or less than the blackest lies. I know him myself now, and his workmen would give their hearts' blood for him, and your words, far from altering my opinion of him, would only raise him in my esteem; for I know from experience the value of your criticisms.' Mary's eyes were flashing fire as she turned. 'Father, have you no spirit left, that you allow your own flesh and blood be made little of this way?'

John McLaughlin looked as if he were going to be determined but, his eyes roving from Maloney to the row of bottles on the dresser, he simply began twisting his fingers nervously.

'Sit down, Mary, sit down. None of this, girl! It's not your place to raise your voice, so sit down. No, go and do what Mr Maloney asked you.'

Mary looked at Maloney with all the scorn she could muster, for her inclination was more to cry than to be scornful, and then snatching a shawl from behind the door she rushed into the yard, to avoid the taunts he was preparing to hurl at he.

'That little girl of yours'll break somebody's heart yet,' said the crony.

'Take care,' said Maloney, 'that her oul heart isn't made bits of glass, John Mack; and if you don't, I'll make it my business to take care.'

'The dog! The stubborn, domineering dog! What business had he to enquire my reasons for coming here? Aye! And to my own face — but I'll make him pay for his interference, see if I don't.'

Poor Mary! The inexpressibly heavy feeling over all the evening had been exaggerated by the words and the coarse stare of the man. If her proud little heart were strong enough to bear poverty, it would not bear to see the father whom she loved and pitied, because of the low station to which he was fallen, degraded enough to yield to this man's evil insinuations.

The parting words of Maloney put the finishing weight to the already overbalanced heart; and tears, which she tried to keep back, would trickle from the dark brown eyes in spite of her. Suddenly, with a start, she realised that a man was advancing towards her, across the heather; and before she could dash away the tears, a well-known voice was sounding in her ears.

'Why Mary, child, what has happened? There hasn't been someone annoying you, has there?'

'Oh no'! she said looking up into Charlie's angry face, 'don't be thinking anyone annoyed me. I am lonely. I have been lonely all day, and I never was so before, so I got sad.'

But what brought Charlie here, of all places, since himself and Mary's father had never been on visiting terms? For Charlie, strictly temperate himself, had an unbounded contempt for the weakness of intemperance in others.

Well, before we can discover his errand – we must, as it is so handy in the imagination to do – go back to the wood farm, in the early hours of the evening in which we find ourselves, when the men had finished their supper and had gone to mitch; and when old Jimmy had taken his chairman's position in the corner, for the purpose of opening the night's debate, and the old mistress had removed her knitting from the satchel at the side of the dresser and had made the preliminary flourishes of the needles while the master had, as usual, stretched himself on the bench in the corner with the head on his arm and his eyes half-closed.

'I am expecting a visit from Miss Briarson soon. Jimmy has just been telling me what he forgot to tell me before: that he was there for a short while and she told him to tell me that I mightn't know the day or the hour she'd come. You know she always likes to give us a surprise that way. I'm glad you thought of it, Jimmy, I must be preparing. It's time for her to think of coming, so it is.'

'And a fine, portly girl she is, too,' said Jimmy. 'It'd put the sight across in you, to see her on the reek, thramin' in the hay, an' pullin' it up, as brave as any o' the men. Lucky the man that gets her, needn't mind about getting knocked up or anything like that, for she'd plough, if it went to that, an' it's a common sayin' that she can go from the spinnin' wheel to the piano.'

Here Jimmy cast a searching look at Charlie to see how he was taking this praise of the girl that the country had long looked upon as his future wife. But Charlie appeared quite unconscious of the conversation. Indeed, but for the movement of his hand, as he stroked Shep's head – who leaned up against him and gazed seriously into the fire – he might be taken for one who had entered the land of dreams. And Eliza bustled about and chatted to Jimmy and Mrs Stuart – her knitting lying in her lap – slept; and the chatterers in turn cast enquiring looks towards the bench where Charlie dozed on, quite oblivious apparently to both the looks and their talk.

'Do you know what it is,' said Jimmy, 'I was just thinking you ought to be the easy man tonight, without that little Miss McLaughlin to scold you.'

'I don't know that,' and the dark eyes were wide awake now. 'I have just been thinking that I am feeling out in the cold, tonight, for want of an argument.'

'Well upon my conscience! She's a terror for convincin' a body, anyway, the devil a better goin'!

'By the holy Father, when she's set herself up to it beyond there, with her head against the partition, it's a counsellor you'd think was in it, if ye shut your eyes. She's a very knowledgeable little girl, an' it's what you wouldn't expect of her with them childish ways of hers.'

A smile was playing over Charlie's face now, and the blue-grey eyes were anything but sleepy; and Eliza was not slow to remark this, as she sat polishing her boots, over against the loft ladder.

'Do you know what it is, Jimmy, you couldn't make head nor tail of her. Sometimes, when I look at her, she appears a child to me. She'll talk to the hens, and the cattle, and to old Shep here, as simple as a three-year-old. And as for flowers, why, she wouldn't let you walk on one for the world. She says she is sure they know these things, when she sees them looking out so happily from the hedge banks. Then against that she'll tighten up her sleeves and work like a woman that'd have a family depending on her. God knows, I pity her, with all her cleverness, and handicapped as she is with that unfortunate father of hers; and I'd interfere, only fearing it would offend her, for she has a strange pride within.'

'But sure ye said nothin' at all about the talk Mr Charlie, and it is the very best thing she's at.

Charlie laughed. 'Oh, you needn't think I could forget that, Jimmy; sure that's what'd put the finishing touch of the puzzle on you. What do you think of her at all? Is she too wise, or too innocent, or too childish, or … There. I can't give you all the ideas I have of her at different times.'

'Do you know my opinion of her?' said Eliza, looking her brother straight in the eyes, as if she would read his very thoughts. 'Do you know my opinion of her? Well, here it is, I think she is a most designing little hypocrite.' Eliza's eyes still remained fixed on her brother's face and she wasn't slow to notice the flush of anger mounting there − a sign that her words had struck very sharply.

'Why do you say that? It's the last thing you could accuse her of.'

'I am not without my reasons for saying so, Charlie.'

But at that instant all further conversation was interrupted by the rattle of wheels in the yard, which woke up Mrs Stuart, and she had Charlie soon on his feet and at the door while Shep dashed into the darkness barking furiously.

'Why, it's Miss Briarson,' cried Eliza, who had been looking through the window. 'Here, Jimmy, scramble down as quick as you can to the forge for one of the men.'

'Well, I'm delighted to be after surprising you again! My dear Charlie! I trust you are well! I'm overjoyed to see you! What a night it is! A starry night for a ramble, Charlie!' And Miss Briarson, rushing into the kitchen, was smothering Mrs Stuart and Eliza with kisses. And there was nothing but confusion in the cottage, what with preparing a bed for the driver, a drink for the horse and a bed for the lady herself; not to mention all the china and silver that had to be taken from this and that and the other corner cupboard and glass case before a table for this visitor could be spread.

'Charlie is not half as much in evidence as he used to be.' Remarked Miss Briarson to Eliza. The fact was that Charlie was so full of the wish to see a certain other visitor enter the farm that he had neither the inclination nor the humour to be overly attentive to this one. And by and by when his mother – coming down from the parlour – whispered that he ought to run across to John McLaughlin's and ask Mary over to give Eliza a helping hand, he acquiesced promptly, though he had Eliza's opinion of Mary fresh in his mind and should not have been so anxious to bring them together. But at this particular time anything at all as an excuse to bring back his tormentor would be agreeable to him.

And soon, with relief, it seemed, at not being obliged to entertain this future wife of his, he was hurrying through the woods.

5

'Nothing has happened to me', said Mary, 'it's only lonely I am.'

'And are you lonely, too, Mary? Why, I was longing for an argument when who should arrive but Miss Briarson, and mother wants you to come over and give a helping hand tonight, if you can.'

Mary's face brightened and her trouble – as is the way of youthful trouble to do – evaporated for the time.

'Of course I can,' and she went in to whisper to her father, who didn't much mind while the bottles were on the dresser, that she was going over to Mrs Stuart for the night. Soon they had left the bog and were hurrying down the shadowy road.

'Old Jimmy was sounding your praises tonight, Mary. Do you know, I am very fond of Jimmy.'

'I am very proud of him too, Charlie, he is such an honest old man. What a pity it was that he lost his leg. But perhaps he wouldn't be as good if he had the power of all his limbs. I remark, when

God inflicts people, he generally pulls up for it by giving them the grace of a resigned and holy disposition.'

Charlie continued to talk of Jimmy, who seemed to have crept into his good graces wonderfully; but soon, alas, he noticed that his eloquence was entirely lost on Mary; for she appeared wrapped in contemplation of the stars, which were singularly bright tonight, notwithstanding the pale light of the new moon.

'A penny for your thoughts, Mary,' he said at last, after gazing for a time at the bright face on which the pale beam fell through the branches, and which was quite unconscious both of the look and of the strange deep light that burned in the dark eyes fixed on it.

'A penny, indeed! They'd be worth more than a penny to you,' said Mary, fixing her dark brown eyes seriously on his face, 'for I have been just remarking how all these stars keep turning round one object – the Sun – and I was thinking how God sees fit in all his works to make a number of things lead up in the end to one. There's an example for you, misguided man, in the stars of the heavens, if nothing else will convince you. See how God makes a multitude subject to one, for their life, light and order.'

'How would it be, do you think, if these stars said to themselves that they could make a better rule than that fixed by the Creator; and went out of their own sphere, to follow new lights?'

'It's just that way with you Protestants, you left the guide God gave, and you are dashing headlong in a pale, outside the ordered condition of things. And but for the far-reaching light and attraction of this despised guide, whom you will not admit, you would run headlong into utter darkness and confusion. How many heads have you at all?'

At this Charlie set up a hearty laugh. 'Well, such a creature as you are! The other night you said I had feet pointing different ways, and now – to finish – how many heads have I?'

'You need not laugh at all. It's a disgrace, so it is. And the family you come from.'

But Charlie had stopped laughing and had paused, with his eyes fixed on her in such a way that it seemed he would read her very heart. And Mary's brown ones, raised enquiringly to his face, noticed a strange grey shadow suddenly cross it in the pale light. Surely it was no trick of the imagination, caused by the moving of branches between them and the crescent moon. No, for his whole attitude bespoke some conflict within.

He seemed as if he were trying to speak, as if there were words struggling for utterance. And still the questioning look in his eyes, and Mary, with a peculiar nervous feeling creeping over her, dreaded those words that might come, and that question in his eyes, having an idea that she could not answer to the satisfaction of the questioner. So, in a hurried tone, as if to break the spell, she said, 'They were a great family in former times – these McLaughlins, weren't they, Charlie? Wouldn't it make your heart bound with pride, to hear the stories old Jimmy can tell about them.'

And Charlie, with an impatient stride, as if angry at his own weakness or whatever it was, laughed in a half-nervous way and said, 'Yes, Mary, they were a thundering lot of terrors, when everyone stood on their corns. I'm not much like them myself, I believe.'

'I do feel very proud when people say I'm a real McLaughlin, as self-willed and proud and as tenacious of right, as e'er a one of them that ever lived. Many a time they mustered on this old wood road, before starting to wreak destruction on some cowardly English robber who wanted to take their lands. And wasn't it some satisfaction for them, to have the exterminators lie awake at night, in dread of their vengeance? It's easy to see the good old stock is gone, when Dick Ratcliffe – that left my poor father homeless, and I might also say soulless – can drive along these roads in his carriage day after day. Oh, that I was born a hundred years ago and that I were a McLaughlin chieftain. Wouldn't I have worked havoc amongst them.'

'Now, Mary,' said Charlie, getting quizzical, 'I don't believe you'd have had a bit of courage. Would you face a regiment of them now, if you had a clan at your back?'

'I'd face anything, I'd …' but at this point she suddenly grasped his arm tightly, pressing against his side so closely that he, not being used to such familiar ways, looked into her face with some astonishment.

'Did you see anything, Charlie? Will you look over there in the side of the wood bank, where the tree is, that the ghost of the old woman does be seen running round. I saw something there just now.' And her hands tightened on his arm.

'Look for yourself, Mary.'

But Mary opened her brown eyes and looked at him with a shudder. 'Wouldn't look for anything.'

Charlie had started another laugh as he said, 'Here's a girl that'd face a regiment; and now she won't look at a poor little rabbit sitting under a bush, in the moonlight, for anything. You're not fit to be a McLaughlin chief after all, Mary. And I for one am glad you waited until this era in our family annals.'

Mary gradually turned her eyes towards the bush and sure enough, there was a bunny, licking his paws under it. With a sigh of relieved fear, her grasp relaxed on Charlie's arm. But she thought, as she looked at him, that he was again going to say that something that she dreaded. So starting off down the hill, she called out to him, 'Who'd be at the gate first?'

'Oh, Mary, with your sense of order in all things, surely you wouldn't start age to run against youth.' But she was gone like a flash, calling back that if the star theory didn't affect him, she'd be on the lookout for another that would.

6

When he reached his farm, she was already hard at work, pouring out tea from the usual earthenware teapot into the state one that only left its place of honour on the parlour sideboard at particular times, like the present. The kettle was singling merrily on the hearthstone and old Jimmy was looking the picture of an easy mind as he watched his favourite, with a smile on his face that said plainer than words, 'You're welcome back, alanna-machree.' And every now and then he would burst forth into 'Oh rowdy dow diddle o de di!' breaking off as quicky as he had commenced.

All this Charlie observed through the kitchen window and the light was in his eyes again, as it had been on the wood road, while he watched that busy little figure flitting here and there and everywhere. And then he proceeded on his nightly tour of inspections through the sleeping inmates of the farmyard.

By and by he ventured in and found Mary and Jimmy discussing the McLaughlins and soon, after finishing a very confidential chat in the parlour, Eliza and Miss Briarson joined the circle around the kitchen fire. Suddenly it struck Charlie that he was beginning to get inhospitable, a failing that had never run in his family, and so, seeing Miss Briarson make room for him, he drew in a chair beside her, looking enviously the while at Mary, who had taken possession of his own special stretcher. Quickly he was monopolised by the visitor and Mary, in the intervals between her discussion with Jimmy, would cast glances towards them.

What a fine girl Miss Briarson was, with her great roll of golden hair and her ivory complexion. Why, she was almost as tall as Charlie himself, and that was saying a good deal. And how they agreed, too. And there wasn't an opinion expressed that she was not in entire sympathy with.

Then Mary pictured what it would be if she herself were in the same position. He wouldn't sit so contentedly, for hadn't he often, after a ten-minute talk with her, stamped his feet on the floor out of sheer vexation at her ideas. But of course, he wouldn't think of stamping his feet at Miss Briarson, and it was really a different matter when he spoke to a highly educated girl in such a position as Miss Briarson held, towards what it was when he amused himself with a child, full of queer notions, such as she, Mary, was.

And she was further satisfied of this when Miss Briarson, noticing in one of her complimentary speeches to Charlie that his attention was wandering elsewhere, had turned to listen; and catching her, Mary, in the act of using one of those pet object lessons from nature, had deliberately told her not to be making a fool of herself. For Charlie had let that quizzical smile play round the corners of his mouth; and Mary, in the light of this new notion that had come to her, put this smile down as proceeding from pleasure at seeing her conquered by this future wife of his.

Then the thought came to her that she was simply there as a sort of servant, to give a helping hand, instead of airing her opinions; and having never compared her work at the farm in this way before, she ceased talking with Jimmy and, leaving the bench, proceeded with the washing up of the china.

But Miss Briarson's pale blue eyes were fixed on her and, presently rising, she said to Eliza that it was impossible for her to remain idle longer.

'You know, Charlie, I'm not used to this kind of thing,' and taking the cloth with which Mary was drying the cups, she said, 'Sit down, dear, I'll do that. I'm no stranger, you know. Don't trouble yourself! I feel it's my business always to help when I'm here.'

And poor Mary, not taken in by the mock softness of her voice, read opposition in the inflection of tone on the 'dear', and in the cold, pale blue eyes foxed so steadily on hers, as if to say, 'you are taking too much time on yourself.' And though she felt like running away from home – anywhere, only out of the reach of those half-closed eyes, with the humour lurking in them – she calmed herself by remembering that Miss Briarson was a visitor. And old Mrs Stuart had called her to herself, noticing the annoyance in her eyes, and kissing her hand had remarked that Mary had given her so much help when there was no one to do anything.

Jimmy too had poked the fire impatiently with his stick, and had thrown his searching look at Mary, and at last had broken into an oration on the great greed of money growing in the world. And this being a pet subject with her, she soon forgot her discomfiture, getting into the old corner beside him.

'Come, Jimmy, and give us a come-all-ye,' said Charlie, at last. 'Miss Emily here is anxious to hear you.'

Jimmy began to draw out all the songs he kept in his old head – as he used to say to himself – and after rowdy-dow-ing over about twenty airs and nodding his head this way and that until they had almost begun to think they would get nothing more substantial, he suddenly burst forth with an old ballad which Charlie described to Miss Briarson as 'a year-and-a-half long', calling on Mary to help him over the chorus.

Then it's oh for the marriage! The marriage
With love and ma bouchal for me
The lady that rides in her carriage
Might envy my marriage to me.

And when at last he came to the end, he put the call on Mary. And she, without hesitation, gave the song he wished for. After that Miss Briarson sang, and Jimmy said afterwards, 'It was all splendid if you could make it out. But sure that was the grandeur of it, and the difference between quality songs, and a come-al-ye.'

Then Miss Briarson, with her usual delicate attention where he was concerned, had requested Charlie to sing; declaring that she never heard a better voice than his, on and off the stage.

'Well, Moll,' he called out, seeing that she had been rather inclined to leave all the talk between himself and Miss Briarson, 'what would you like me to sing?'

'Oh,' said Mary with a straight look from the brown eyes, 'don't ask my liking about it. Sing what pleases yourself.'

Soon Charlie's rich, deep voice was making the rafters ring with his favourite.

> *The night is falling fast,*
> *And I'm thinking of the past,*
> *As I'm sitting, with my darling by my side.*
> *She's an old and wrinkled dame,*
> *But I love her just the same*
> *As the sunny day she came to be my bride*

And soon Mary, forgetting the grudge she owed him, was joining heartily in the chorus.

> *'Tis the dear old cabin!*
> *'Tis my own old cabin!*
> *'Tis my home, on my native shore.*
> *I will give my latest sigh!*
> *I have lived and I will die!*
> *In the cabin with the roses at the door.*

Miss Briarson was smiling all the time, for wasn't she beside him, and wasn't it in compliment to her he sang it. And Mary knew that, too, but it didn't keep her from joining in the chorus all the same.

And old Jimmy, why, he was casting his sharp look from one to another and perhaps it rested longer, and with more enquiry, on Charlie than on the others; for there was exultation in Miss Briarson's eyes, and it made him poke the fire impatiently, and there was musical enthusiasm in Mary's brown eyes as she beat her small feet in time and humoured the time with her hand. But in Charlie's eyes, there was something which old Jimmy couldn't understand.

That deep light he had noticed in them was puzzling him, for Jimmy was well versed in many things, from experience in his wandering life. And this light had kindled up a notion in the old man's mind which, it must be said, was pleasant to him and yet it was a perplexing notion, too. For could this be really the same matter-of-fact farmer he had known from childhood?

7

Mary agra! Your soft brown eyes,
Has willed my fate, he whispered lowly
J.K. Casey

So the night passed and Mary remembered it like the first night. She had felt out of place at the farm, for she had placed in that impressionable mind of hers many words and actions that had passed there. She saw them in a new light, during the long hours she lay awake pondering them in her mind and listening to the drip, drip of the April night shower against the window panes and the solemn tick of the grandfather clock, and the winds sighing away in the fir trees − sounds that had heretofore been the sweetest music, lulling her to sleep, and that were more precious to that imaginative disposition than the softest strains that had ever echoed through the palaces of kings, but which went, on her last night at the farm, almost unheeded.

Perhaps the thing that stung her the most was not that the future mistress of the cottage had treated her contemptuously, or that Charlie had taken pleasure in this contempt, but that, in the conversation of the previous night, she had remarked that Miss Briarson, agreeing with him on every subject, seemed no way put out by his religious views. On the contrary, when some such subject had cropped up, brought into the foreground by Charlie himself for the purpose of drawing Mary out − as she was bound to be drawn out on that point – Miss Briarson had not only smiled contemptuously at her objections but had not made a single stand herself, in spite of the religion she had professed. Maloney's' words came back to her:

'Oh, the devil a turn, ever he'll turn, and they say she doesn't much mind herself; all she wants is the boy.'

Mary's heart was sore, for she knew the craving in his old mother's heart and noticed her pained expression at Miss Briarson's carelessness. Yes, it was out of pity and love for the old woman she had left herself open to contempt and given him cause for amusement. What was she, more than a fool, to imagine she could succeed where Father John, and even his own mother and his dying father had failed. But he would amuse himself no more with her, she would stop at home for the future, and make the best of it.

But there was another watcher in the old cottage during these long hours, and if the thoughts running in his mind had been thrown to Mary, which alas they were not, it might have saved many a heartache in the days to some.

This watcher was none other than Charlie, who sat at the little window up in the eaves of the farmhouse, looking out at the waving trees in the wood. And what is Charlie doing here? Charlie who never let 10 o'clock see him in the land of wakefulness.

'To think,' he said, 'that I could care as much! I that never cast a second thought on any woman living. It was only tonight, when I missed her merry laugh, and her thousand little joyful changeable ways, that I knew what she was to me. My dear little girl that pities the woman that'll get me and tells me there's no love lost between us. And perhaps she's right, too, not to care for an old fogey such as I am and yet I keep dreaming, when I may guess the awakening that's to come. I wonder could she ever begin to care for me? But no! Didn't she say herself she could never disagree with the man she'd love and aren't we always quarrelling? And yet I ought to chance it. I know Eliza wants that fortune she never got, and there'll be wigs on the green between her and me if I do not marry her favourite. But let there be! I'll never marry my girl for her money! I'll never marry at all, if I don't get the one girl in the world for me. And yet, I dread to chance it! I dread to break the friendly relations between us by offering what I am sure she will refuse.

'I wonder is it true what they say – that she secretly encourages Maloney, on account of his wealth. But I'll not believe it. I couldn't believe that of Mary, Mary that says what she thinks, and tells my faults to my face. What a contrast to Miss Briarson, with her sweet tongue, and her entire agreement with every opinion, good or bad, I care to utter. She is too agreeable to be genuine, I'm afraid.

'Give me the girl that says what she thinks, in spite of everyone. Oh, my dear, proud, provoking little girl that had to be reminded of her position here tonight. How I longed – the while I had to smile at her indignation – to stand up and, drawing her to my side, tell her that she was no stranger here, that she never would be a stranger to my heart or home.

'But enough of this wavering. I have spoken tonight, and tomorrow she must give me my answer, be it good or bad.'

8

There was great fuss in the kitchen when Mary came down next morning. Mrs Stuart was preparing to start for town, and old Jimmy was departing for Kilgorman to spend a few days with an old friend, before starting on a round of wandering, which would very likely take him the biggest part of two years to perform. Jimmy was up betimes that morning, for wasn't Kilgorman eight miles away, and wasn't it a hard day's work for him to scramble that far?

'When will you come home again, Jimmy?' Mrs Stuart was saying as she stuffed a parcel of bread and meat into the old man's pocket.

'The Lord preserve you and yours, ma'am, until this time two years when, if I'm still alive, I'll be there to see the champions hid. I'll be passin' back though in a week, but I won't come in. I'll just take a look over the hedge above, at the rye that Mister Charlie is goin' to sow today.'

'Well, you'll be welcome any time to come, Jimmy; both for your own sake and the sake of the man that brought you here first. God save you now.'

'God be between ye an' harm, ma'am. Where's Miss Mary? Sure, I couldn't go without sayin' good-bye to her.'

Mary was soon in the foreground and taking the old man's hand she led him up the hill.

'God be good to you now, Miss Mary; you're doing good work below. Keep at it, acushla,' and with that Jimmy disappeared round the turn.

When Mary got back to the farm breakfast was going on, as Mrs Stuart was in a hurry to start for town and Charlie was anxious to start the planting of the rye, for there were clouds gathering over Knockastia these days, which boded ill for the weather. Soon Jack Martin had the journey's cart ready, and was pulled up before the door, in all the glory of a new frieze suit, while he cracked the whip and settled the reins, and called the pony pet names and abusive ones in turn. The while he imagined to himself that he was just as fine a fellow as Dick Ratcliffe's coachman, if he only had the livery.

Then Mrs Stuart appeared with Charlie minus his headgear, following to help her into the car and settle the rugs around her; for no one ever dared take that job out of Charlie's hands, whatever might be the hurry. And Miss Briarson was out, too, and throwing condemning looks at Mary for her temerity in helping to make Mrs Stuart comfortable.

'Did you see the new cushions I made myself?' said Mrs Stuart somewhat proudly to Miss Briarson.

'Listen to this now,' said Charlie. 'How she prides herself. If I began to talk that way, you'd see how she'd cut me up.'

'And Mrs Stuart has a good right to pride herself on her work,' said Miss Briarson, 'for where would you see such a collection of house linen as she has?'

'Don't apply the word "see" to other hoardings. Sure they were never made to be seen. Their one purpose in life is to afford sustenance to future generations of moths.' Charlie was taking a turn of teasing his mother and Mrs Start knew well what he was up to, so she smiled while he continued, 'Mother thinks there's none such as herself.'

'Wait till you get as good,' said Mary, taking his banter somewhat seriously.

'I'll be bringing in one that will be twice as good as ever you were, Mother, in a few days more,' and he gave a sly look at Mary, which didn't seem to please Miss Briarson, for she turned impatiently into the cottage while Charlie went out to the gate to wave his hand to his mother as she turned the crossroads.

It wasn't long till Charlie too was gone to his business and then Mary felt lonely indeed. In spite of her efforts to get away home, Mrs Stuart had persuaded her to remain for the day and finish some repairs on a cloak while she was away. So now she set to work in earnest, for she had the place to herself, Miss Briarson and Eliza having one of their confidential chats in the parlour.

'Did you observe it, Eliza, before last night? Why I wasn't half an hour in the house before I saw through her plans. You know yourself that Charlie is soft enough, in spite of his business-like ways, and it seems to me this designing creature has been trying to entrap him under your very nose. You must be very dull. I declare I saw through it all the first letter I got from your mother, describing her perfections; and that's what has me here. Your mother must have been very foolish to allow this forward piece to enter the house.'

'Well, I never saw a bit of what was going forward until I got that letter of yours. I've been a bit observant since, and I think she must be what you say. At all events, I saw plainly yesterday evening that she has come round Charlie. I wish you had seen his face when I gave my opinion of her.'

'No person could be so innocent in ways as she pretends to be. I'm sure she's a hypocrite.

And seeing, Eliza Stuart, that your brother was taken with her, how, in the name of all that's' wonderful, did you continue to bear with her?'

'What could I do? Sure, I couldn't tell her to go out of the house.'

'Oh, my dear woman, there's many a way of killing a dog, besides choking him with butter, couldn't you insult her, for a beginning? And if that didn't take – which I guess it wouldn't – what harm would it be, for the ultimate good of all concerned, to concoct some story? Have you ever heard anything about her you could build on?'

'Well yes, and I have, since getting your letter, taken advantage of it, too, but without any apparent success. There's talk about herself and the fellow that came home from Australia with them. I can't say whether it's true or false, but I have come around it to Charlie. I tell you, Emily, it'd be better to raise your hand and give him a slap in the face than to mention it. I wouldn't venture it again, that's all.'

'I know, Eliza, it's plain to be seen she has enticed Charlie. If there had been any promise from him to me, I'd hold him to it; and you see yourself all the good that marriage between us would effect, and all I could then do for you …

along with my frequent visits here that have given the people room to say that such a marriage was contemplated. Now that this person has sighted big game she will follow it up. But leave her to me. I have dealt with too many girls since I took to housekeeping not to be able to manage this sample.'

And a look shot from Miss Briarson's eyes, which, if Eliza had had the sense to read, would have shown her that she too would be dealt with properly if ever the time for such things came.

Mary was busily engaged when Miss Briarson entered the 'end room' and when she lifted her eyes an involuntary feeling of admiration stole over her at the stately figure and fair face of the visitor. But her admiration was soon checked by the harsh tone of the lady as she exclaimed, 'Go on with your work girl, and don't be so curious,' fixing her cold eyes on Mary the while.

Now if it had been an open attack, Mary would have entered the challenge unhesitatingly. As it was, a sharp pang at this unmerited rebuke shot through her, but she remained silent while Miss Briarson cast about for some excuse to thwart her, and presently letting her eyes fall on some parings scattered about the floor, she said, 'You are very untidy. Have you no consideration for the hard-worked girl that has kept everything going. If people were made to clean up after themselves they'd be more careful. Pick these up, girl.'

The McLaughlin spirit was gradually rising in Mary, for she began to see that it was simply a spiteful desire to annoy her that animated Miss Briarson, and as all the colour faded from her face she tried to control herself sufficiently to give a proper answer, when Eliza called from the kitchen.

'Are you there Emily? I want you.'

So poor Mary was left to calm herself, as well as she could; and when she had got her temper so much under control as to begin to rebuke herself for being too toucheous and to think that Miss Briarson could be actually like that − a lady of her means and background. Sure wasn't she used to working in fine houses and dealing with people of different stations. And such is life.

'I must keep things to myself,' said Mary aloud as she continued about her work. Her lot was not to question. And even if she did, she couldn't even see through Miss Briarson's strange ways, couldn't unscramble what she was about. Until suddenly, as she moved towards the kitchen to collect her shawl from behind the door, she overheard some interesting conversations.

'... well, what do you think? The plan could work. After all she wouldn't be happy here and certainly Charlie couldn't be putting up with her strange ways. She's much too cheeky and coarse for a man of his means.'

Eliza replied, 'Well, I'm not so sure.'

'The girl is shrewd. It's clear she is after his money. Well. I mean someone of her station is always looking to better herself. Now what do we know about developments with this other fellow, Maloney? Surely we could move things along there?'

With that, Mary decided that it was time to leave. For one thing she didn't like to eavesdrop. And secondly, she did not want to get embroiled in any conflict where Charlie was concerned, much less Mrs Stuart. And besides, they were probably right.

'Sure maybe I have notions above my station. But Charlie, he must be thinking about me or else why would these two women be conniving in such a manner? Still, I know Charlie, he won't let these women control him. He's his own man. And isn't that's why I admire him so much?'

By this stage Mary had reached her home and decided an early night was in order. But still she couldn't believe what she had heard that afternoon and found it difficult to lie still in bed. Over and over again she thought to herself … so they think I'm too cheeky and coarse. Now what could they mean by that? And just what were they planning to happen with that old fogey Maloney, the man with the red eyes and wisps of hair falling over his face?

'Now that's coarseness for you,' said Mary, 'what with all those rings on his fingers – "the fellow with the cuthriments" as the others called him.'

Again, a strange feeling of depression stole over Mary that made her feel twice as anxious as before. She thought of the day when her very own father had admonished her for speaking her mind in front of Maloney. "It's not your place to raise your voice. Do what Mr Maloney asked you."'

She was determined that no one would take charge of her destiny. By now Mary had slipped into her own dream world, a world far different from her simple surroundings – fresh linen tablecloths, saucers and cups, silver spoons, a different dress for every day (always white), starched collars and cuffs … but then she was woken by a loud knocking in her door.

'Mary, Mary, are you there?'

Now who could this be? And at this hour of the morning, for it was pitch dark outside. It sounded like Charlie, but why would he be calling at this time of the night? With that she got up and went to the door.

'Mary, we need you now. You must come over. It's Miss Briarson.'

Miss Briarson...' She was about to say something else but then she remembered what Miss Briarson had said about her being coarse and decided not to say anything more. Mary also remembered the conversation from that afternoon. So this is it. This is Eliza and herself up to their connivance. But what could it mean?

'She called for Eliza and when Eliza got to her room, she was gone ... and in my home. Mary, I couldn't even bring myself to go to the room, but my mother asked that you come over to help. She only feels comfortable when you are around.'

Now Mary was given to grave feelings of guilt.

'How could I think even such a thing of this poor woman? Sure wasn't she kindness itself, always helping out Mrs Stuart and Eliza, and then coming out to help out poor Charlie.'

With that Mary grabbed her black shawl and wrapped it over her small shoulders and went with Charlie. 'Strange', she thought, 'Charlie seemed very different, but maybe I shouldn't read too much into what he is saying at the moment. He's probably suffering from shock. And it's only natural that he should be feeling such.'

Then a new twist came about in this tale. For Charlie took Mary's right hand gently as he took her through the haggart and still held on to her hand when she was safely over the stile.

'Mary, you didn't say anything to upset poor Miss Briarson this morning? I know that you can be a little too direct at times. It's just that she seemed so jovial this morning.'

'Say anything to her? You know I couldn't get a word in edgeways. If anything, I'm the one who should be upset after the things she said about me. But for now, I keep my mouth shut. My father always told me no to speak evil of the dead.'

Charlie ignored these comments, deciding not to pursue this line of conversation. Instead he said to her, 'You know, Mary, you are quite a hand about the house, and I think my mother would like to see much more of you.'

'Charlie, what are you trying to say to me, sure amn't I always down with you and helping out when I can?'

'You're right, you're right as always. There's something else I wanted to say but for the moment the words are not coming out and you are not helping, either.' With that he squeezed her little hand more tightly, as if that very gesture should say what he had in his mind.

'Sure I'm only trying to ask you in a roundabout way if ....you'd be ... or rather consider ... or think about being my ... good ... wife?' Charlie didn't wait for an answer from Mary and immediately went on to say, 'Now you don't have to give me an answer immediately. But tonight, after all this, I decided to ask you directly. And you know, Mary, it's so much easier in the dark, for if you say no you won't be able to see the sadness on my face.'

It was the last statement that threw Mary, for never before had Charlie shown such frank emotion.

'Now Charlie, it's the shock of what happened to poor Miss Briarson that's affecting you in this manner. Sure, she's the woman you should have asked, and all this drama would not have come about. But what does Mrs Stuart say to all this?

And maybe you're asking me all this because you've just lost your chance with Miss Briarson and I'm second choice.'

As soon as she said those words, she knew she shouldn't have uttered them. For she was a complete bundle of nerves and in her frame of mind she was no longer conscious of what she was saying. For once Mary McLaughlin couldn't be direct. She wanted to say yes but couldn't bring herself to say the word.

'Mary McLaughlin, how many times have I tried to approach you in the past few months to ask for your hand in marriage and you in your inimitable way gave me no opportunity to do so? In fact, I thought you were playing hard to get. And now this concern about my mother. Isn't it you I'm asking and not my mother? But you know what she thinks of you anyway. You know, Mary McLaughlin, I think its compliments you're after now.'

'Well, I'll be damned. You know I never in my wildest dreams thought you'd put such a proposal to me. But I also think you know what my answer is. So I am not going to give it to you now. It just wouldn't be right. Let's tend to Miss Briarson. This is not a time for proposing, with poor Miss Briarson laid out in your very own house. Let's talk about it in two or three days' time, when all of this is past. And by the way, I want to talk to you in the light of day for I want to see the expression in your face as I give you my answer.'

'Well, Mary McLaughlin, there's no doubt about it, you're quite a little trickster. Someday I'll tell you about this very evening and about things that will bring a little smile to your face. But as always, you're right. Let's go to the house. I'm sure they are wondering what's keeping us.'

Eliza was already standing at the door when they arrived.

'Oh, Charlie, I'm glad you're back. She's all right. A miracle! It's the doctor we'll be needing now, for I think it's her poor heart that's affected. She has just spoken to me and the first words on her lips were ... "Charlie, where's Charlie Stuart? It's Charlie I need. He should be here by my side ..." Now Charlie, the first thing you should do is go in and see her, say something to her that'll cheer her up. And sure I don't have to tell you what to say. You should have said it long ago. Now you have the ideal opportunity. Be gentle with her. Then go down the road for the doctor. Now there's no time to waste.'

Believing that she had now done her bit in the matchmaking process, she turned then to Mary.

'Mary, girl, as for you, go and make a pot of tea for all of us, for that is what we need to keep us going. We need to get us over this terrible day, and when you have finished that, you can go and give poor Miss Briarson a cool washdown, for I'm sure her temperature is too high ... but wait 'til Mr Stuart has finished his business. He should be on his own. Now off with you.'

Charlie looked to Mary and, smiling, gave her a quick wink, which said more than a thousand words. Mary turned to him and said, 'Well, maybe I will give you my answer tomorrow, Charlie.'

They then both went about their instructed ways.

By the following morning Miss Briarson had made a remarkable recovery, for she was seen leaving the Stuarts' home, bag in hand, as dawn broke. Just what Charlie said to her as she lay sick in her bed that early morning, we will never know. But one thing is certain, and that is that she left the Stuart home with what can only be described as an aggrieved heart.

Fate has a strange way of working.

When Molly was in the Ribbonmen

By Francis O'Fiachran

(Nora Feehan)

What was the attraction that drew half the bone and sinew of the parish to Farrelly's cabin on winter's nights, when the summer's saving would be flaming and roaring and making war with the bog wind in the big chimney? Or on summer eves when they should be wielding the 'camán' or landing the football over the hill, for the honour and glory of the old country? Was it the bits of information that Dillon was in the habit of dispensing at the top of his voice from the *Independent* as he lay in the open settle bed after the day's work? Or was it for a share of the viands that his sister Molly prepared in plenty for the supper, and to which every comer, rich or poor, young or old, was so welcome? Or, 'likeliest thing', you will say — was it for a share in the affection of Molly herself? Well, about that last consideration I'm in doubt.

For Molly was an old maid, though the name doesn't seem, now it's written, to express her at all. I won't say that. Would 'bachelor girl' do? Worse. Molly was one of the stout, jolly, strong-armed colleens that used to foot turf on the bog, do a man's work and dance at the crossroads forty years ago through the waves of time. She was good-humoured, tough but with the light still in her honest grey eyes and a laugh that would make the ashes dance on the hearthstone. For my own part, I think the attraction was in her tongue, for once she started, Molly would make the round of the country and come back to where she began, telling stories of bad and good, of all the people she knew. And now that she is gone, God rest her, the very 'seanthus' in Farrelly's cabin is no more.

One ambition Molly had, and that was to identify with the Ribbonmen[1] of old. Give a hint that you thought that she was as good as a Ribbonman herself in her young days, and you paid her the highest compliment.

'Ach,' said Molly to me one summer's evening as she filled a great mug with tea for Willeen from the saucepan, 'ach what's the world comin'

---

[1] Irish Catholic sectarian secret-society movement that was established at the beginning of the 19th century in opposition to the Protestant Orangemen.

to at all. But sure it couldn't come to anything else with all the fine, brave, spunky fellows run out o' the country like redshanks and nothing left but 'spalpeens' of shop boys wheelin' about on the rheumatic tyre.'

At this, William gave a 'haw, haw' from the settle bed that had the tea going the wrong way.

'Bravo, Molly, sorra lie it but they are rheumatic, I always had them doctored.'

'You're not much better yerself, you impudent little puckhaine. What interrupting you have. Only for my old grandfather Jack Gilligan leavin' me to you on his deathbed, it's your coffin you'd be in. For sure none of the women that's goin' would ever cook for you the way I did, and sure it was the weight of the responsibility an' you, when you were two years old, that made the poor old man kick the bucket for good an' all.'

'Molly,' says he, 'take the weight of that fellow off my conscience before I die and cook the bit for him and wet the pinsheen of tea and bury him decent out of your own pocket when he goes, for,' says he, 'the sorra he won't be long in it but long or short keep him from the shulers and women that's goin'; for they're getting good for nothin' but reading novels.'

'Molly,' says Willeen, 'do you remember the time you thought you were chattin' Peddher Reddy?'

'Musha why wouldn't I remember it? I was a little runner goin' to school at the time but I don't deny it, I was a bit of a smirk an' Peddhereen wasn't the only one I thought I was chattin', for I used to carry on powerful with every bloomin' Ribbonman, and I had a couple of polis after me as well. But no, it was Peddher I had the *gradh* for.

'Well it turned out that there was to be a big flare-up beyond at Brogan's in Clonfad and the whole band were to be at it, an' what would you have but me, brave Molly, should be in the thick of them.

"Now, Molly," says my grandfather. "Titivate yourself to the nines and put on a clean bib an' be a credit to the house you're leavin'."

'And with that he ups and takes out his great new red-spotted Sunday handkerchief an' dips it in the nog o' Bulmer's, and dickens such a scrubbing I got before nor since. After that he dives into his britches pocket. "Here Molly," says he, "and let it never be said that Jack Gilligan didn't behave decent when he ought. Here Molly's two ha'pence to tip the piper."

'Well an' good there was one – a huggadha of a fellow – an' he was gone stark starin' out of his mind about me. An' in a fit of divelment I gave him the word to take me to the dance an' of course Peddher, on account of thinkin' he was chattin' me, come too. There were two big box bushes outside our door and I told Molloy to get into the middle of one of them, 'till I was into my dancin' rig-out, for if me grandfather as much as got a sneeze of what was goin' on, we were all done. An' he had a great fashion of goin' to the door every other minute to see what colour of clouds were goin' down after the sun, for he was as good as a weather glass.

'Well by and bye, up came my bould Peddher, an' it put the heart across in me with joy to see him out through the window. He fires his legs across the wall an' ducks into the other box bush, an' sure it was the mercy of heaven he didn't go into the wall where Molloy was or they'd sweep one another from the face of the earth till there wouldn't be as much as a bit o' their hide left to identify them at the inquest. By and by Peddhereen rose to see if me grandfather was lookin' an' at the same time Molloy rose too. An' when they got a sight o' one another, you'd never do a day's good if you seen the faces of them –

all as one as if they were the Pyramids of Egypt. Only for the *gradh* they had for me they'd a been wigs on the green. As it was, they rose every time me grandfather went in an' sparred an' ground their teeth at each other like game cocks.

"Molly," says me grandfather, just as I was going to start. "Hand me down that crangers, for I see a stump beyond in the top of the box bush an' I'll clip it before night falls."

"Wait till tomorrow, " says I, but me heart was gone down to my heels for I knew it was the top of Peddher's head, as he was too tall to get himself down the whole way in the bush.

"Sorra save the wait," says he, for with Jack Gilligan to say such a thing is to do it on the spot, and with that he seized the crangers and made for the bush. What was I to do? Was poor Peddher to be scalped before me eyes? And then me grandfather hated the Ribbonmen, and if he found one o' them was makin' eyes at me, his granddaughter, he'd get up that high that there was no knowin' what he'd do.

"Grandfather," says I, "grandfather," says I again. And then such a palaver as I set up never was heard. "I'm after seein' a sprit in that other box bush. For God's sake grandfather, run and lay him and don't have him appearin' before me face."

With that me grandfather looked and of course when poor Molloy heard me shoutin' and saw me grandfather lookin' and havin' the crangers he began to crawl out o' the bush as hard as he could.

"What," says me grandfather, "what – Pauddheen Molloy's son – curse that was left on ould Paudheen for his villainy, making poetry in his young days. Let me at him, the beggarly ould yahoo! Comin' about my place and makin' rabuses about my child – but I'll make the rabusing out of you!"

And me grandfather made one charge for Molloy just as he went head foremost out of the bush an' made a clip at him that sent me bawlin' for help to Peddher. Molloy faced a thorn hedge and cleared it but me grandfather cleared it just as quick and as they disappeared over the bog, myself and Peddher took the shortcut to the Brogans.

"What do you mean, Molly, by puttin' Molloy there?" says he when we were well into the bog with all the keenawauns noddin' at us from the pools.

"No matter what I meant, Peddher," says I, "but I wouldn't put Duke Wellington in your place."

"That's all well and good," says he, "but if your grandfather had come to my bush that time, I'd exchange places with any duke that ever swum. But let that pass," says he, an' with that he looked at me an' I looked into the bog holes.

'And that,' said Molly, turning to me, 'that'd show up the different rarin' we got them days. It wouldn't be the girls that are goin' now that'd do what I done. The love was comin' out o' that fellow's eye that strong that you could light a match at it, and what did I do? I looked down at the shadows o' the keenawauns dancin' in the bog holes.'

'Tare-an-ownthers an' thunder and turf, Molly,' said Willeen, 'an' how did you see the bonfire in his eye if you didn't look at him?'

'Is that all your newspaper readin' does for you?' said Molly. 'Didn't I give you the ins and outs of it? Didn't I see his shadow below in the bog hole the other side of keenawauns, that's how I seen it.'

'Bravo again, Molly, when I'm goin' to bring home the woman I'll know where to put the question, anyway.'

'Brogan's was worth lookin' at that night. The pewter plates on the dresser were like rows of full moons, they were that polished, an' the flitches o' bacon was shakin' the loft with the force o' keepin' themselves up. An' the fire was roarin' like a bull up the chimney an' a clamp o' turf in the corner with Hugheen Garry tunin' his fiddle on the top of it to be out o' the dancers' way.

'Arra there's where you'd see the sportin' an' the fine rosy-cheeked portly girls with drugget petticoats on them an' maybe I wasn't second to the first o' them myself, for Peddher turns to me an' says he: "Molly, it wouldn't be gother 'hideout you but let us not be savin' o' the flure while it's in it. I dance to you Miss," says he, making the prettiest bow. An' sure all I wanted at the time was the win o' the word when I was waiting it away before him.

'My grandfather was fit to be tied afterwards when I brought him back the two ha'pence but what could I do when Peddher behaved decent for me and him every time the music rose? Well no, I don't deny it but though we were a sort of chain, he never spoke up straight to me, so when the dancin' was in full swing an' when he comes and sits down beside me in the corner I knew what was comin'.

"Molly," says he.

"Yes," says I.

"Me an' you were always ..."

"Froth an' we were, an' that's the truth, Peddher," says I, "an' we always ..."

"Not a word o' lie in it," say he, "an' there to be a meetin'," says he, "and I'll ..."

"You will," says I. "Arra don't be tellin' me, Peddher," says I, "sure you were always ..."

"Aye, was I," says he, "– sure me feathers always rose when I ..."

"I don't wonder at it," says I; "but did you hear...?"

"Every mortal word of it," says he, "but sure Molly," says he, turnin' the back of his hand at me, "there's no use tellin' you any more of it. You know more than the Captain himself."

'And so I did, too, an' only for the information I gave Peddher that night he'd be pickin' oakum this forty-odd year instead of lying clean an' decent beyond in Amerikay. Well I looked up at Peddher then ...'

'I suppose,' interrupted Willeen at this point, 'I suppose there wasn't any convenient bog hole to look down at.'

'Never mind you, now' said Molly, 'you had no experience of those things for I always kept an eye on you. As I was sayin', I looked at Peddher an' I tell you my heart leapt out of me mouth at the minute, for I know what was comin'.'

"Molly," says he, "look over there between Jim Whelan and Tommy Mahon an' tell me is that Molloy's leg I see goin' where they're dancin' the jog. He must have escaped your grandfather," says he, "but no matter for that, Moll," says he, "for it has nothin' to do with me an' you an' what I'm goin' to say. But wait," says he. "I've a word to say to the Captain over here." So off he went and with the colloquin' they had I was left without my dance for a good ten minutes.'

'Musha sorra such dry love-makin' as that ever I heard,' said Willeen.

'Not a word out of you, didn't I say before there were none o' that curse-'pon-your-sow, you-love-me carryins on in my day. Poor Molloy was up in his bonnet anyway, an' well becomes him if he didn't begin to show off, singin' some of ould Paudheen's makeup, an' this is the way it went.'

Here Molly began to sing in a mincing time:

Here's to the cock that crew.
That weakened the people in France
I'll cut the tale o' the whale
An' make the Black Hack for t' dance

'But Peddhereen cut him out black by singin' that his own grandfather made, an' it brought down the house for it had us French in it but was a fine decent song about our own townland where we were all herded and rared.'

There was Hughy Garry from Clonfad
An' Feery down the Fann
They dance a double hornpipe
At the sale o' those young lambs
An' there wore bidders gather 'her
But the sportin' lads of sweet Clonfad
They far surpassed them all.

'On the minute, a reel was formed, an' in the middle of the hullabaloo the song raised, Peddhereen rushed up to me with the hair fairly standin' on his head with excitement.

"Dance this last dance with me, Molly," says he, an' away we went and all of a sudden he gave me one swing round the kitchen an' when I lit on my feet he made me fall on my nose with a slap of a kiss. An' on the minute out went every candle in the place.'

'Haw, haw, haw,' laughed Willeen from the settle bed, 'that was a strong one anyway, Molly, couldn't ye's go a little milder and not leave the decent neighbours in the dark with the strength o' your affection.'

'Go long out o' that sure it wasn't the kiss put out the candle, you sprahaun, you. But never mind,' said Molly, laughing. 'Never mind if there wasn't the pullin' an' haulin' a before the candle were lit again. When the light went up sorra trace o' a man was to be seen in the place but one of the tails of a body coat that I held onto. I dunno whether it was Peddher's or no but anyway I kept it ever since in remembrance of him. Well becomes me, brave Molly, anyhow, but when I went to bed that night what did I do but begin to dream. I thought there was a hole in the wall beside the bed an' out of it were comin' a long line o' pluvers[2] an' I squeezin' them as hard as I

---

[2] Believed to be birds

could but sure I couldn't squeeze them as fast as they come.

"Musha Moll," says me ould grandfather next mornin', "what kind o' shurauns were you goin' on with last night."

With that I ups an' tells him the whole dream. He sat down with his hands in his hair thinkin' for a long time when all at once he turns around.

"Molly," says he "you'll hear somethin' you won't like before long" an' true for him the very next day there was a hullabaloo over the country. It seems the boys went off after the lights were put out down somewhere near Beggar's Bridge to a big meetin' an' bedad they were all but caught an' the very time I was squeezing the pluvers they had the oul Captain himself outside our gate wounded and were just a hair's breadth of bringing him in, for which me grandfather was never done prayin'; that they changed their mind and brought him to a loft over Robert's barn beyond in Clonhugh in which the polls catch him through watchin' the doctor.

"And what of Peddher?" I asked. "Sure, himself an' the rest of the boys had to fly to America after." An' I never saw his face again. He died about a fortnight after landin'.'

'And were you sorry for him, Moll?'

'Musha sorra bit, the little puckain.' Here Molly considered a little. 'Oh, faith, I was sorry after,' said she. 'I made him a present of a silk hankercheer goin' and I was sorry it was gone for nothin'.'

At this Molly laughed, but in the pause that followed she stuck the tail of her praskun to her eye in a furtive way.

'Molly,' said Willeen, breaking the silence. 'Molly do ye know what I'd be thinking of?'

'What?'

'I wonder did Reddy give you as good a squeeze as you gave the pluvers?'

The Widow and the Sweep

By Nora Feehan

1

Larry Farrell sat on the big tailor's table in his
brother Jim's kitchen, sewing buttons and putting
braiding on the rig-outs of half the country. He
was one of those people who, having been set
down by circumstances, in a particular walk
in life, remain fixed there for good. Had some
volcanic upheaval suddenly occurred under Jim
Farrell's cabin, shooting Larry to the world's
end, we have no doubt but that, if any spark of
life remained in him, he would inevitably have
crept back, by hook or by crook, to his original
position; and seated cross-legged on the edge of
the crater which had engulfed his abode, would −
if orders were short − have cut the buttons out of
his own breeches, and have sewn them on again.
People winked at one another, and whispered
that Jim was cute enough not to let Larry get any
higher than the button sewing, afraid he'd set
up in opposition, but it did not seem as if Larry
himself ever thought of such a thing.

Yet Jim had his own reasons for keeping Larry in complete ignorance of the noble art of 'cutting out'. He knew that there was always danger, more especially when the pension age would have arrived (*mar, de reir mar a bhionn said as airig cun aoise is amhlais a bionn said ag airig nios measa*), of that extraordinary upheaval of human nature known as 'love' intervening to shatter the ligaments binding Larry to his table. Yet the danger seemed ephemeral, for Larry's brain had always been so chock-full of buttons and button holes that there did not seem a likelihood of any woman− granting her to be so inclined − pushing her way through to his heart. Jim had a wife and a family, but that was all 'in the course o' nature', just as it was for him − Larry − to sit on Jim's table and stitch, and if it was 'in the course o' nature' for him to 'change his life' sometime, why of course, it would all come round 'in the course o' nature' without his bothering himself to get off the table at all.

So Larry pegged away − his mouth puckering in sympathy with every picker he made in the cloth, and his frosty beard going up with every draw of the needle.

'Here, Larry,' said Jim Farrell, giving the finishing touch with his goose[3] on a waistcoat. 'Here, Larry, take a run over to the Newlands with this suit of Master Harry's, an' if there's any alterations to be done, be sure an' take a note of it. Hurry into your Sunday duds, an' make haste, for I see Croughan Hill lookin' blue, an' that's a bad sign.'

'Smash it,' said Larry, swinging himself off the table. 'I wouldn't wish for anythin', that I had to leave them buttons before I had them finished; an' I think I'll never be back soon enough to see how they'll look, when they're all in'.

Ah! Little did Larry know that the relationship between him and his brother's table had been dissolved, 'in the course o' nature'.

Soon Larry found himself on the way to Newlands, footing it along with short jerky steps and looking more 'Jack Frosty' than usual amid the budding life of the early spring. No use, young primrose, in your making eyes at him through the ivy tangle. No occasion, Violet, for your hiding behind the leaves so demurely; he is not going to pay any heed to you, for his head is full of buttons, bachelor and otherwise, so full

---

[3] A tailor's goose, an iron.

indeed, that it takes a splatter and a splash of raindrops, and a trickle down the back of his neck to arouse his attention; and then he looks, first in apprehension, at the blue-black rain cloud over the treetops; next in despair at the carefully pressed crease down the front of his 'bran'-new' trousers; and lastly in desperation at the house of the Widow Mulready, over beside the big wall of Newlands.

He humped himself up under a hedge, but it was not fully fledged yet, and the new leaves, disturbed, shed limpid drops over him, so that the 'bran'-new' trousers were getting uncomfortably sprinkled, not to mention Master Harry's suit in its brown paper parcel.

'Anythin' for the sake of appearance,' cried Larry, making a rush for the widow's door, scrambling over her flower pots, and puffing and blowing into her kitchen, where he stood, dabbing the raindrops off his trousers, and screwing himself round to see if the back of it had got any.

'Blow that rain! Am I much wet, Mrs Mulready?'

'Oh! Not a bit at all, Mr Farrell. You'll be as dry as a lime kiln in no time!' exclaimed the widow, taking a turn around him, and giving an odd flick of her apron here and there.

'Wait now! Stand easy, a mhic! There's a little stream here on the back of your collar,' and the widow carefully rubbed the back of Jim's neck with the corner of her apron.

'Sit down here now, in the corner, and take a heat of the fire; sure what great hurry are you in; till the cloud passes over,' said she, 'and I'll wet a drop of tea for me and you, comfortable-like together.'

With that the widow took down a nice blue teapot from the white dresser, and while she prepared the tea, Larry took out his specs and put them on; and then he remarked that there was a bunch of bachelor's button flowers on the table; and he remarked too, that the widow's cheeks were as the flowers; and that she had two of the funniest brown eyes in the world, and no streak of grey in her black hair.

'Be the dang, but!' exclaimed Larry, as he sat with his hands on his knees, staring hard at her, while she wet the tea, and turned the quarters of potato cake on the griddle.

Slowly his eyes wandered in a wondering kind of way up and down the tidy kitchen, from rafters to floor, till they reached the big window with the well-scoured table under it, and there they rested, up and down between the table and the window in a comparing stare. All at once he gave the table a terrible blow with his open hand, which had such an effect on the Widow Mulready that it almost ended the triumphal career of the blue teapot.

'Smash the lie on it!' he exclaimed again as if a sudden convincing thought had struck him.

'Aye, an' dash the lie on it!' said he with still greater emphasis, staring hard at the widow as she handed him a mug of fragrant tea and a steaming plate of cake.

'An' blow and take all the buttons in Ireland!' he said, turning his eyes to the bunch of bachelor's buttons, 'blow and take all the buttons that were ever buttoned, but the buttons there on your table, an' the buttons in your cake, Mrs Mulready – I – I mean the – the blushes, ma'am.'

Larry commenced at this to drink the tea in hurried mouthfuls, while the widow sipped hers bashfully.

'Mrs Mulready,' said he, after looking over the specs at her for another start, 'Mrs Mulready! A tradesman's a tradesman, when all's said an' done; and if it was in the course o' nature for a widow woman to marry a threadsman that could sew in buttons − I mean a tradesman that could sew − could make trousers with bachelor's buttons, dash it! I mean bachelor's buttons, I mean somethin' ma'am, an' I can't say it because I never done anythin' but sew buttons; but I'll learn, so I will'.

The widow put up her apron to her face to hide her blushes.

'Indeed, Mr Farrell − Larry − I'm not much good at givin' lessons, so I'm not, but sure all I know −' 'What would you know, ma'am, about the cut of a trouser, though if you would like to give a helping hand at the stitchin', I'll not be one to stop you'.

'Oh, I thought it was others sorts of lessons, Mr Larry. I thought − I think I thought you didn't know how to say − to say it, an' havin' experience, I was goin' to −'

But the widow did not get any farther, for at that instant the door was suddenly flung open and a couple of barefooted gossoons, followed by a little girl, rushed in.

'Oh! Mother,' cried one of them, 'we had a great time in school. The master was watchin' up the road from the window all day, an' every bike that'd pass he'd say, "Is that a telegram?" Some of the big lads were saying it's what he was lookin' out to see if he was gettin' the sweep.'

'Isn't it well,' exclaimed the widow, in a new tone of voice, 'isn't it well for some people that's paid for doin' nothing? If he wanted a sweep, he could get plenty of both sweeps an' tinkers round the Half Moon down there; a decent person can't see the door with them, from one end of the day to the other — sweeps indeed! Purty connections!'

'Be the dang!' exclaimed Larry, the eye almost leaping out of his head with alarm as three youngsters suddenly laid hands on and wouldn't let him 'hear his ears'.

'Be quiet children! An' listen for a minute,' cried the blushing widow, as she noted Larry's sudden perturbation, 'not a word! You are goin' to have — Mr Farrell — Larry — will I tell them what they are goin' to have? You were just sayin'...'

'Be the dang, but! I never said anythin', ma'am!' And Larry bounced up nervously. 'Oh! The dickens a ha'porth ever I said. Did I say anything?' And with that this incorrigible trifler put the specs in his pocket, took Master Harry's brown paper parcel under his arm, shot out of the widow's door like a stone from a catapult back the way he had come, forgetting his errand to Newlands.

'The purtiest little woman! An' kind; but be the dang, but! I was all but marryin' the children, unbeknownst to myself.'

2

It was not till Larry had entered his brother's kitchen that it came to him he had let his narrow escape from the above-mentioned calamity occupy his thoughts so far as to cause him to leave his errand unexecuted; but Jim was so excited over some news that for once he did not give him a rating on his absentmindedness.

'Larry,' he exclaimed, 'Master Harry has sent over word that you had a share in a ticket which has drawn a horse in the Grand National Sweep. Now, as Molly here says, where on God's earth would you get money to gamble, unless you stole it out of the brown jug where she keeps the coppers? So she thinks that it must be us that won it, as it was our money.'

'No, Jim', said Larry, 'it wasn't your money, or Molly's, either; because it was the half-crown that Master Harry gave me for a Christmas box; an' when I was lookin' at it in my hand, he says maybe I ought to try my luck with it on the National, and "Do," says I, an' that's how it was.'

'Well Larry, it's proud I am this day, that you have an opportunity at last, of making some restitution to me for all I have done for an' taught you, not to mention the little woman herself here.'

Larry looked at them both, and sorrow for them, then, that the Widow Mulready had knocked the buttons out of him, so to speak; for as he looked, the hump of stitchery between his shoulders began suddenly to straighten out, so that by the time he had finished looking at them, he had become as straight as a crowbar while he absolutely swelled with importance.

'No more buttons for me, Jim, because I'm beginning to think it's the dickens of a trade you're obligatin' with me. Here goes for £200 an' a farmer's daughter an' the back of my hand to you an' Molly,' and with that Larry took the road.

'What's come over him at all, the unnatural little leprechaun,' cried Jim, 'him that was always so biddable, an' content there on the table. He must be gone stark starin' out of his mind.'

'Oh! Let him go, the creature,' said the wife, 'the news of the money was too much for him. He'll come back by and by when the rain washes the conceit out of him.'

But neither of them knew that the Widow Mulready had put the 'come hither' on Larry, and that he'd never be the same man again.

3

When Larry found himself once more in the rain he began to think.

'The widow's a purty little woman, an' kind — be the holy farmer! She's all that an' there's no mistake about it, but she's only a washerwoman when all's said; and with a fortune I ought to marry a fortune, an' not a houseful of children that'd smother your head talkin'.'

As he trotted along at the rate of six miles an hour, muttering to himself, he went slap into a big fellow, who came bursting though the hawthorn hedge by the side of the road, bringing with him a plenteous supply of raindrops from the young leaves.

'Ara, Larry Farrell, is it out washing the cobwebs off yourself you are?'

'No! Joe, but what has me out is this – I feel somethin' here – for somebody. An' be the dang, but the washerwoman would make a purty little wife ... but maybe I'd be better off with a farmer's daughter. Did you read on the paper that I'm after winnin' the whole National, for a horse? I suppose I'm valued for upwards of three hundred or maybe more – I haven't found out yet. Never say again that Larry Farrell is not an independent man.'

Joe Reddy opened his eyes very wide and commenced staring at the tailor as if he imagined him to have suddenly gone off his head.

'I've left Jim's house because to put them all in a nutshell, they're nothin' but a fighting crowd; an' whatever sort of woman you get for me, don't get a woman like Jim's Molly. Will you side me up, Joe?'

All at once, Joe saw how the land lay, and a look of harmless villainy shot into his eyes.

'I'm your man, Larry.'

'Done,' cried Larry, stretching out his hand.

'Leave it there, Joe.'

'Had you e'er a little girl in your eyes, Larry?' said Joe, when the handshaking had concluded.

'Why me eye's so full of this minute that I can't see a stim. There's one, an' she's powerful, but there's encumbrances there, Joe, an' leaving her on one side, the next best is Kitty Coffey.'

Now the mention of Kitty Coffey staggered Mister Joe, for she had been his sweetheart from the days when he helped her to carry a sod of turf to school, and it was said that it's before the priest he'd have brought her long ago, only that her father had the word on him for a play actor and a playboy. Not that he hadn't been cheeky enough with his new acres, to ask the strong farmer for his little girl.

'I'm your man, Larry,' said Joe again, but are you sure no one is coddin' you over winnin' this money?'

'Codding me, is it? Begad it was no cod when it was on Master Harry's paper, because Mr Harry pays dear, for 'is paper. It wasn't the same news that could be on it as a cheap paper like the *Independent*.'

'Well then Larry say nothin' until you get the cash; and then we'll swear in a few stout lads; an' if Coffey doesn't agree to give you Kitty by fair means, we'll have an abduction.'

'Oh, delays are dangerous,' said Larry. 'So I'll call round an' borrow fifty pound from Billy the Bum, on the strength of what's comin', an' when Coffey sees the cash flaughoolah with me, it'll clinch the whole business.'

The next Sunday evening when Kitty went walking down by the wall of woodlands, Joe Reddy wasn't far off; and if they didn't laugh immoderately, well leave it there!

4

The stout fellows had been sworn in, and on the important occasion, Larry had stood treat handsomely, as could be judged by the remnants of a pretty extensive supper scattered about on the table in Joe Reddy's bachelor's quarters. As for Larry himself, Joe had him, as he said, 'titivated up to the nines' in plus fours, clock socks, patent dancing shoes and other incongruities, which had the effect of making him look quite eldritch.

'Now boys,' said Joe, 'one more pound from P. & H Egan of Tullamore, for there's a dreadful ordeal before our friend Larry here. It's an ordeal we all have to go through nowadays, if we want to get work on the road and a cottage house.'

'Joe,' interrupted Larry, 'I hope you're not alludin' to me, as my fortune's made, by that blessed sweep, whoever he was. But, if it was a thing that I was a road man I'd take it easy, if I were yous, on every day of the week, except the Friday before Saturday, when the overseein' man does be knocking about.'

At this there was a hearty laugh from the boys, and when it subsided Joe continued.

'Yes, Larry, we all have to go through it sometime or other; an' some gets through it handy, an' some maybe gets the kick through it, an' them last is the lads that has to get another try. I nearly got through it myself several times, but never came to my destiny, by reason of the father, when I'd be drawin' up to it, callin' for a butt of a candle to go to bed. One night I nearly got up to it, an' I know I'd have got the kick through, only he had his boots polished, an' up on the hurl ready for the fair of Ballyboggan the next mornin'; for stockin' feet, he knew, would come off second best against my hide. But I'll be at him again.

'Now Larry keep the top of your head up, an' when you come to Coffey, step in about the floor, like the Lord Mayor, an' says you to old Bill: "Everybody cannot live in solly-tairy-ness, God forbid they should; so I've thrown my eye this while back, an' by your leave, on your daughter Kitty."

'An' then Larry, on the spot, whip out a handful of silver – and while you're speakin', keep jerkin' back an' forward from your waist up, as if you couldn't get all the words that was in you out easy – whip out a handful of silver, an', to cut the ground from under old Bill altogether – says you, "Is there any dogs here will eat money? Aye! Or cats or pigs, or other domestics of that kind? For I've lashins an' lavins for man an' beast, with a sweep on the National; an' I belong to a fine long-tailed old family, a family with a tail so long that it'd stretch from Hell to Connacht; and here I am, an' I'm goin' to remain."

'Have ye's any doubt it? 'An' then Larry, get up a sort of witchman's antics; spin three times round the kitchen on your heel; wave your hands over Kitty, an' beckon her to follow you; an' we'll be outside to back you. It won't be hard to put the heart across in old Bill, because he had a sister once that nearly died on the head of an' old witchman makin' love to her an' you look for all the world like him.'

'Come on boys, like men,' cried Larry, too excited over the result of his adventure to remark the doubtful compliment paid him by Joe, 'come on,' cried he, seizing his hat, and making a rush for the door. 'I'm hot on it this minute an' I'll never draw my breath again, in peace an' ease, till I'm engaged to her.'

Larry went like a hare at first, nodding his head emphatically over what he was going to say; but as they drew near Coffey's he began to slow, so that when they arrived outside the gate he was very much in the rear.

'Come on now, Larry, an' be a man,' said Joe, 'I'll raise the latch for you, an' after you have done as I told you, if old Bill refuses his consent, we'll be outside here to do your biddin'.'

'Oh Joe, give me time to draw my breath – oh Joe, I can't go because me heart's after goin' down, for he's a dangerous man, I often heard it said; an' a champion wrestler – oh, Joe.'

'Come on out of that, haven't you the fortune he's lookin' for. The witchman's antics will tame him soon enough. Take it Larry, like a dose of physics. Mind now I'm goin' to raise the latch.'

'Oh be the dang but don't, Joe. All the spunk is after goin' out of me, by reason of his being such a dangerous man. Come on back to your house for another crapper of P. & H. Egan, and then we'll come back an' I'll go in.'

'Come on, I tell you,' cried Joe, as Larry made a sudden rush for the stile they had come through. 'Stop him boys, stop him.'

And Larry was soon captured and brought back. 'It's now or never, with you,' said Joe. 'Brave it man alive, brave it!' and opening the door he gave Larry a push that landed him right in the middle of the kitchen floor.

There was no going back for him now, so he commenced trying to bring his heart up from wherever it had gone down to.

'Aha!' exclaimed Bill Coffey, a great heavily built, red-faced man with grey side-whiskers, smoking in his armchair by the hearth.

'News of my coat at last, I often heard tell that it takes twenty tailors to make one man; but what's a tailor made of? There's a question for yous. Lies, lies, nothin' but lies. Every tailor is a whole ramshackle of lies.'

Here Larry spied Kitty, sitting demurely in the corner, an' as she caught his eye she gave him such a beaming smile that he plucked up some little courage in his heart in spite of the witherin' choleric state her father had fixed on him.

'Mr Coffey,' said he in a quaking voice, 'everybody cannot live in – in – in–'

'But what the dickens are you tryin' to say?'

'In – in – in solly – solly – tairy – ness, God forbid they should,' stuttered Larry, making a spasmodic butt.

'Soly-tairy-ness,' exclaimed Bill Coffer, 'what does he mean, Kitty? Maybe it's a new-fangled name for nakedness, an' that he's going to close upon my coat.'

'Mr Coffey,' said Larry, getting more courageous every time Kitty smiled at him. 'I don't know much about myself, but people do be telling me I'm a fine grand shape of a man, as any girl–'

'Tare an' ages!' burst forth Bill Coffey as he bent forward in his chair, took the pipe from between his lips and fastened his eyes on Larry.

'–as any girl might wish for in a husband. With a trade in my fingers, an' the sweep at my back, I make bould to throw my eye on–'

'Oh, me. Larry says it's on me,' cried Kitty, rushing over and throwing her two arms round Larry's neck.

'Him! What! Thunder an' turf! Girl, you're daft. Oh, the Lord between us an' harm! What's that?'

For an ululation like the cry of a banshee suddenly filled the kitchen from rafters to floor.

'Oh Father,' cried Kitty, starting to sob, with the corner of her apron pressed to her eyes with one hand while she affectionately circled Larry's neck with the other.

'Oh Father, it's the fairies that's callin' me to follow him over the hill an' dale. An' you'll have to give me your consent to marry him. Oh don't be cruel an' say you won't.'

While Kitty was crying, Larry was going on with the witchman's antics and calling for dogs to come and eat the handfuls of silver he was throwing about the kitchen.

'Oh lord, oh lord,' cried Bill distractedly. 'Is the curse goin' to light on us again?'

'I'll have to have him, Father, an' don't call for a butt of a candle, for you called once too often.'

Here Larry started receding towards the door, beckoning to Kitty, who seem too bewitched and compelled to follow him, while a blood-curdling ululation, apparently coming from the fire, resolved itself into some sort of incantation:

Ochon, a pee
Come marry me,
Or bring red ruin
On your father

Bill Coffey sat, thunderstruck, with the fate of his sister running through his mind. Certainly Larry looked eldritch, as he hopped backwards towards the door, with the bewitched Kitty following. But he could not see her enticed away without making some effort to break the spell, and just when Larry had reached the threshold he was upon them. Seizing the departing Kitty, and finding himself in close proximity to her swain, anger got the better of his dread of witchery and, lifting his foot, he gave the charmer one kick that landed him, in a series of staggers, clean across the yard and over the stile while he locked and barred the door to secure the bewitched and distracted Kitty.

5

Larry was giving his supporters another of many suppers the following night and all were seated round the board awaiting the arrival of Joe Reddy, who had undertaken to act as a middleman between the Coffeys and Larry.

'Boys, oh boys! Hadn't I the sink to talk up to him the way I did! And to think that the lovely little darlin' wanted nobody but me all the time, unbeknownst to the world,' Joe exclaimed to himself.

Here the latch was raised and Joe, looking fit to burst with excitement and joy, entered the kitchen.

'Well, Joe,' said Jim Daly, 'I suppose you have it all settled, and the match made.'

At this Joe threw himself back in a chair and laughed and laughed till he had the whole company in stitches, Larry laughing loudest of all.

'Yes, Jim, the match is made, all right,' said Joe, laughing while he spoke, 'but in a way you'd never guess. When I went in Kitty started bawling and the old fellow said she'd been at it all day. I tell you, his eyes began to shine when he saw me coming in.

"Reddy," said he, standing up and holding out his hand, "leave it there; a man and a decent whole man." But Kitty cried, "Oh! don't be talkin, sure what is he to my Larry?" Well, he recounted all that had passed the previous night, his hand one side of his mouth, the way Kitty wouldn't hear him; the same as if I didn't hear every word of it up the chimney. "Now, look here!" said I to him, "Your girl has got crazed about Farrell, and I'd let her have him, if I was you, for he's a dangerous man, with a power of money he got the charms on the sweep men, an' it would be your advantage to keep the short side of him.'"

With that he considered a long time and, "Reddy," says he, "it's quare for you to be talkin' for him, you that was so gone on her yourself one time."

"Oh!" said I, "that's all a thing of the past now, for no one would like to interfere with a witchman, or he will have his way, in spite of you and me."

"Oh! Woe, woe! The fool that I was to stand in the way of a fine decent boy that knows how to plough and sow. Oh! Four and twenty tailors, went to catch a snail … Reddy, will you risk it an' take her, an' I'll sign you over the whole concern?"

"Well," said I, "as I said before, no one likes gettin' in the way of a witchman, but it's said if anyone could turn the girl's thoughts from him, the spell would be broke."

"For God's sake, try," says he.

"I will, an' welcome," says I, not dreaming how things were goin' to turn out, Larry. "Anythin'," says I, squeezing the old fellow's hand for the sake of auld lang syne. An' Larry would you believe it? I was whisperin' with Kitty there in the corner, on one stool, an' puttin' in good words for you, an hour an' a half, when the spell was broke, an' no one would do her but myself; and before the old man called for the butt of a candle, he had me tied up for good. But Larry wasn't the grandest part of it all, the way the 'gradh' fell in me, when it left hers for you.'

Larry found it hard to agree with Joe's philosophy, but he could hardly bear any ill-will, seeing Joe was immediately on the look-out for another match for him. So the suppers went on, while Larry and his party took the round of every farmer's house in the country and outside it — he getting the kick-out so often that his coattails were becoming threadbare from the dint of application.

But if the star had sunk below the horizon, without a shadow of doubt that of his busy guard seemed to be ascending by leaps and bounds, for they were doing better for themselves than for the man they were out to help get a wife.

Jim Daly, on one 'turas', started pleading Larry's cause with so much vehemence that, as he said himself, he got all mixed up and put in his own name where he meant to have put Larry's so that, he being a handsome boy and the lady thinking he spoke in his own cause, she accepted him on the spot. Then, just when the 'fortune' was in the way of having its effect on a rather mercenary young lady, Tom Clarke had to butt in by falling in love with her and so depriving Larry through his ardent wooing of the one real chance that came his way.

There was dead silence in Joe Reddy' kitchen on the night Tom Clarke invited the whole party to his wedding. At length Joe arose, rather shamefaced, to toast the successful wooer.

'Well,' said he. 'That we may win another hundred, along with the hundreds we're gettin'; an' that Larry here may get one of the bridesmaids, an' win the Derby Sweep.'

'Sweep! Sweep!' Thundered Larry, rising suddenly from the table, 'may the d… sweep the whole lot of yous out of the country. Yous are all marryin', the course o' nature for me will be to marry the childhre', so wheugh!' said he, making one bounce out on the door.

'When all fruit fails, here goes for Mulready.'

The Prelude

By Francis O'Fiachran

(Nora Feehan)

They had, of course, done their fair share of building air castles in those glorious days. Ted would find gold in Klondike or diamonds on South Africa and with Mr Ellis's blessing he would live happily ever after. But girls of nineteen and boys of twenty-one are generally content with the goods the gods allow and Ted had dallied on until Mr Ellis's scathing final remarks had at last opened his eyes to a sense of his prospects and duty. Poor Ted — down in Mabel's heart dwelt the thought that their daydreams might yet be realised. Someday her hero would return triumphantly and bear her away in spite of worldly uncles and all that kept them apart. Hope is one of youth's privileges. The paths trod by youthful feet, be they ever so dark, have yet the distant gleam of coming sunshine to relieve them. Despair waits for a riper age and for eyes that see not the hereafter when earthly prospects fail.

So Mabel wandered on through the woodland path, dreaming of future happiness and drinking in the pleasures of the waning day, which had ceased to drip. The air was fresh and fragrant and down the green distance came the thrushes' evening song, chorused by a medley of lesser bird voices. Soon she reached a little brown stream down between the steep banks and here, scrambling to the water's edge, she sat on a rock ledge over which the ivy trailed to the water beneath. Yes, he was very serious that day when they had sat there together two years ago and had stumbled through his first declaration of love. Serious — how funny it was even to think of Ted as serious for once. Poor Ted, she thought. Where is he now? Will I ever see him again and will I ever learn to forget him, if not? A noise of bursting branches on the other bank caused her to look up suddenly and then an exclamation broke from her: 'Ted.' Yes, it was he, springing across the chasm that divided them.

'Mabel, my darling, at long last.'

Was it Ted who held her in a warm embrace or was it only a part of her dreaming? She lifted her eyes to his face.

'Yes. It is really you, Ted.'

'Really me, Mabel, come back once more – the prodigal again, and you have thought of me all the time, Mabel. Why, I had ceased to hope, but finding myself once more in the old place I came surreptitiously to visit this old dell, the place I have dreamt of many a night, wandering up and down the world. Do you keep a corner in your thoughts for that summer evening two years ago when we sat together here?'

'Always, Ted.'

They clasped hands and sat silently looking down at the brown water. At last he broke the silence.

'Take all the pleasure of all the spheres and multiply, this is heaven for us, Mabel.'

'You have grown serious, Ted.'

'Yes, it has been well battered into my numbskull these last two years. Serious, but not rich, and you will scarcely believe me when you I tell you that I have tried to clutch at riches as a drowning man clutches at a straw, Mabel. That weapon alone can cut down the opposition of your uncle. In the past two years I have bobbed over pretty well all the oceans on the face of the globe in pursuit of the fickle goddess. At the end of the period, behold me, poorer than ever, more in love than ever and more reckless, else why have I tempted fate by coming home?'

'Don't talk about it, Ted. Let us just be for this evening, be as we used to be, let us forget poverty, opposition, everything, and be just two sillies.'

'Yes, it was easy that time, but I think, as you said, I have grown serious and cannot take things as I could then. That long period of absence from you set my brain working towards a particular point and it is hard to get out of worrying and thinking, even with you here beside me.'

Mabel's fingers pressed closely on his as she said, 'Then don't think anything, Ted, but this: all the fickle goddess could send me would not pay for the joy of your coming home today. Let us forget her place and where she has been. Will you ever forget that sight, Ted? Picture to yourself uncle pushing her up the tailboard, one of his inimitable feats.'

Ted lay back against the ivy-clad bank and roared.

'The first hearty laugh I had since that never-to-be-forgotten day. Its ludicrousness was eclipsed in my mind by the finale. This one idea has had a hold of my brain since then. Has that lordling or professional ever turned up? I have pictured him in my dreams, and he has become a living reality to me, the object of rancorous animosity. How many times have I broken the fifth and every other precept with regard to that pince-nez-wearing, spindle-shanked, straw-haired …? I am positively afraid to start on a string of descriptive adjectives qualifying him, particularly in the company of a lady.'

Mabel laughed.

'He is an accomplished fact, Ted. He is a Siamese twin, as in fact there is two of him in it.'

'Only tell me where to find the monster.' Ted made as if to start to his feet.

'Just as bad as ever. Sit down, you silly boy, and let us be thoughtful for a little till I explain. And now for the full, true and particular history of the Siamese twins. You see, just recently a new doctor and a new solicitor have come to town. They are inseparable chums, have thoughts in common (aspirations and affection) and they have set them on poor me. The doctor is by no means spindle-shanked, is son and heir to that famous court physician Sir Silas Banders, and has a glorious medical career opening before him, or so he says. The solicitor is a nephew of the most noted judge on the Woolsack, with talents and wonderful prospects of success. Both have captured the fancy of uncle; both have placed their whole affection on me; he declares both have his approval, etc., etc., etc. A fancy-dress party is being given over yonder in our house two nights hence. They are coming. I am supposed to accept whichever offers me his hand and prospects first. So the gods, in the person of uncle, have decreed.'

'And the gods in the person of Ted have decreed otherwise. I am going to that ball, Mabel.'

'You dare not, Ted; uncle would recognise you.'

'Yes, the fiat has gone forth that I am going in the guise of Brutus — the impersonation of revenge, rage, jealousy, etc. Going to put my foot in it or on it. I would not ask if you favour their suit.'

'By no means, Ted, but if you will come do try to prevent the popping of the question by either of them. But for goodness' sake don't ruin the situation as you did once before.'

'No, once bitten, always shy. I shall take good care and then the fun of it will be the satiating of my long-fostered passion for revenge again that beastly two-headed Hydra: professional success. We shall have our own little share of happiness.'

'But how do you intend to get in?'

'Oh, I shall stalk in the shadow of those Siamese twins. I feel a curious sensation, as if they were leprechauns destined to lead me to buried treasure, or something of that kind, when I have given them a good squeezing, in every sense of the word. Yes, expect me as the avenging angel in some of the guises under which he has appeared on the unfortunate planet. But in the meantime, the golden moments are flying in which we have each other alone. Let us take them and forget the Hydra. Let it be old time, old dreams, again.'

So they wandered away into the green woods of spring, swinging each other's hands and dreaming the dreams that only come in the springtime of youth and love.

A Historic Fancy Dress

By Francis O'Fiachran

(Nora Feehan)

A rumble and rush of carriages and motors, a shaking out of drapes, a bloom in mirrors, a fluttering of gauze, a hint of perfume. Many curious glances. In the midst of it all, looking quite at sea and making the most ridiculous mistakes, is Mr Ellis. Dancing has started and the ballroom looks a veritable scene from a fairyland, with pageantry from ancient history. King Charles the First is there, flirting outrageously and irreverently with his grandmother, the Queen of Scots. Charles the Second, too, is hobnobbing with Anne Boleyn under the very eyes of Henry the Eighth. William and James are glowering at each other — not over the Boyne but over the golden head of Queen Victoria, at her coming to the throne.

The guests are yet arriving. A dumpy and fat-legged Napoleon, accompanied by Charlemagne, present themselves before Mr Ellis and give greeting. Following them and gliding past unnoticed in the confusion of recognition goes Brutus. Mabel, chatting yonder with some ancient and much exposed grandmothers, notices him. A smile not caused by the caustic remarks of the ancient dames flits across her face. She is attired as Desdemona and looks the character to perfection. Presently, Charlemagne arrives, hard-pressed by Napoleon – née the doctor.

'May I crave the favour of your fair hand in the coming dance, fair lady?' Charlemagne bows so low that his extended military headgear comes in violent conflict with Napoleon's waistcoat, chucking out the rival's request for a dance in a spasmodic and gramaphonical manner.

'Pardon, Madame Desdemona, I protest. I am before him. I requested the favour and was granted it yesterday.'

'The deuce you did.' A fight between the two emperors seems imminent.

'What business have you— oh hang it, who's this?' Brutus stalks forward and, taking Miss Ellis's arm, waltzes with her. Napoleon and Charlemagne join forces for the time being, and both make as if to chase the pair.

'Who the deuce is … yes, who the deuce, Pluto or the Hangman? Which?' demands Napoleon, while a laugh, politely concealed, runs round the ring of the matrons' silence.

'Don't display your plebeian origins, emperor, have you never been to a Shakespearian play? That is Brutus, wearing a black mask.'

In the meantime, Mabel is laughing immodestly with her Shakespearian partner and many eyes are following them as they whirl along through the opening waltz. Napoleon and Charlemagne, crestfallen and dejected, eye them moodily from the side of the room, both being too thoroughly disappointed to seek a partner elsewhere.

'Who the deuce is he, anyway?' asks Napoleon, again. 'The bloke waltzes divinely and Mabel seems to be on remarkably pleasant terms with him.'

'How did you manage everything, Ted?' asks Mabel.

'Oh, quite easily. I sneaked in on the rear of the Siamese twins. They monopolised uncle immediately, so it was only common politeness to move.'

'But you are most remarkable, Ted, and I will not fail to notice that you have not paid your *dettes*, as *le docteur* over beyond would say.'

'The fates be propitious to me and keep me from paying any such debt. I have only two debts oppressing my conscience just now. One, a personal account of two years' standing regarding that unlucky night between Ted Warren and Miss Mabel Ellis. High time it were balanced. The other, a debt which ambition has opened and which I must close. Come hither and let me repay my mortified spirit and forever owe you for it … for the manner of my entry.'

Through the folding doors leading to the conservatory they pass and presently emerge after a long promenade down the palm-shaded dimly lit corridor onto the terrace beyond, to where the shrubbery trees cast long shadows in the moonlight, where Ted's character slips away.

'At last, dear love,' he says, clasping her and pressing his lips to her hair again and again.

'Look up at me Mabel, dearest. I want to see your dear eyes answer, as well as your lips. The question I am going to ask: do you love me enough to follow me out of this luxury and affluence to follow me, Ted Warren, the scrivener, the outcast, the chauffeur, the vagabond? Will you leave your uncle's home and come to me, as I am? I did not dare to ask this before, but honour has been chased away by the pain of absence. Will you marry me as I am, and share my poverty?'

She raises her head from his shoulder and, fixing her blue eyes on his dark ones, speaks, while his heart seems to hang on her words.

'With a heart new fired I follow you, to do I know not what, but it is sufficient that Brutus leads me on.'

And then for a long time there is silence between them, heart speaking to heart in the embrace of their betrothal. Presently, a footstep breaks in upon the lover's rhapsody and Napoleon's portly figure appears on the gravelled walk at the outskirts of the shrubbery.

'We are discovered, the *docteur* will tell all to uncle. Run round up the path, dearest, while I keep the sawbones at bay.'

And with a spring forward, Ted confronts the amazed Napoleon in a melodramatic attitude: 'Get you to bed, yin, it is not day. Is not tomorrow, boy, the ides of March?' And then plucking at his scabbard he adds, 'Let's carve him up like a dish fit for the gods.'[4]

But the emperor waits to hear no more. The retreat from Moscow is nothing to the undignified scramble of the sham emperor. Making a rush for the conservatory he takes flight for the ballroom,

---

[4] Quotes from Julius Caesar

colliding at the entrance with the solicitor and rolling over and over among the dancers. Brutus, emerging on one side and seeing the gasping Napoleon, throws out his hands and exclaims in awestruck tones: 'Tis very like; he hath the falling sickness!'

A suppressed titter circles through the crowd of spectators and then from the upper end of the room Mabel comes in, leaning on the arm of her uncle. The doctor, still gasping for breath, is leaning against the wall while the solicitor is berating him soundly.

'Why in heaven's name, man, do you rush like a sledgehammer or Halley's comet at the fellow? If you are disposed to get rid of your adipose tissue, at least do not overburden others with its ponderousness.'

The poor doctor sympathises with Mabel: 'Mabel, have you seen a spirit? You really look *Les Misérables.*

'*Oui*, Madame went *à la promenade en que vive* the fairest and most *magnifique* of created beings and instead had a *rencontre* with Monsieur le Diable, minus the culminating points.'

Pardon, ma belle enfant. This is our dance,' replies the doctor.

The waltz is rather a strain on the doctor, who takes all his time to keep in step, particularly with such a small and willing partner, and he is just incapable of talking on any subject save one.

'Ye gods, what a piercing black eye that Brutus chap has, he seems non compos mentis. Do you know him? He looms *à la française*. We have been introduced to him and travelled for some time in his company.'

'Really'? *Mon oncle* requested the pleasure of an introduction from me just now, he said he understood he was of our party. (Mabel's cheeks became like June sunrises). As I was not aware of his identity, I could not do the job, however, so you must introduce me so that I can fulfil Mr Ellis's request that we meet. He particularly asked me to make him aware of his identity. Here are both coming near us. Now allow me *le plaisir* of an introduction all round. Let us take a stroll through the conservatory first.'

And Mabel half drags the doctor towards the folding doors to avoid the dreaded *contretemps*. Ted adroitly darts to one side, out of view of Mr Ellis. But she knows, as the doctor presses her arm while pacing between the great palms and exotics, that it is out of the frying pan and into the fire with her.

The doctor's face is absolutely gleaming like a moon. His smile will not be repressed. What an opportunity! What a game fate has played into his hands. Tom, with all his law and order, with his vaunted smart ways, will not outdo him. What is there to be done but to open his hand, or rather his mouth, to gain the much coveted and beauteous prize. But another thing remains to be done. A dim and wavering light − but the words he had conned so strenuously from the French books and dog-eared grammar of student days are lacking. The doctor gets desperate. She is showing signs of flight as the words in his brain appear in his unwilling cheeks and compressed lips, so he falls on his knees before her, pinning her into a corner.

'*La rose à la terre*. Allow me to express my ...'

'Really I am so sorry you should have slipped.' Mabel in an agony of fear, lest the dreaded proposal should take place, seizes him by the arm. 'Allow me to help you to your feet. I trust there is no serious injury, doctor. Let me go and find uncle.'

But the doctor, getting to his feet and keeping her in the corner with great difficulty, seizes her arm and exclaims, 'Allow me to express *la passion* I feel. For ... for some claret cup.'

'Yes, I know your weakness, doctor, let me fetch some. You really must be injured seriously about the knees. The fall was so great. Almost as great as that of the prototype − in a different sense, of course.'

'Allow me to express myself. Do not request my *ascension*. I would prefer to grovel before you, *la Rose magnifique*, than to rise to the dignity of him whom I impersonate, in part successfully. I flatter myself. Allow me to *descendre* once more.'

And the doctor sinks to his knees, imagining himself as Napoleon must have looked before Josephine in his prime.

Suddenly he rebounds and, turning on his heels as on a pivot, stares in horror as Ted, who has come up behind, strutting an attitude, exclaims: 'How ill this taper burns. Ha, who comes here? I think it is the weakness of mine eyes. That shapes this monstrous apparition. It comes upon me.—Art thou any thing? Art thou some god, some angel, or some devil That makes my blood cold and my hair to stare? Speak to me what thou art.'

Napoleon stares spellbound at Ted, who strikes an attitude of unbounded horror.

'Nay press not so upon me. Stand far off. Away slight man, thou monstrous apparition.'

This is enough, coupled with Mabel's laugh, to stir Napoleon to his deepest depths. His native language disappears, as if by magic. 'You confounded ..., looking like a blackamoor,' he exclaims and rushes on. 'I'll teach you not to come sticking your club foot between me and the lady of my choice.'

'And what if the lady of your choice chooses to cast herself into the arms of your enemy?'

The doctor turns to behold in the distance Mr Ellis' approval, while Mabel is nowhere to be seen.

'Your Josephine has departed down yonder corridor with your archenemy and bosom friend. Fly while there is yet time, before they exile you to St Helena.'

Forgetful of his spleen against Brutus, the doctor rushes madly towards the passage, ignoring Mr Ellis's evident desire to be introduced to Brutus, who flies in his wake, disappearing through a window. He is in time to escape, as a Mr Ellis reaches the turn that would bring him into view.

As for poor Mabel, in rushing from one evil she has again fallen into the clutches of another. With her uncle advancing and eager for an introduction to Ted, she deems herself happy when the solicitor, entering the ballroom, claims the pleasure of her company on the terrace. She trembles as she leans on his arm. Surely her uncle will recognise Ted, his disguise is such a thin veneer. How easy to discover him by his swinging gait, his voice, his mannerisms, his eyes, in a conversational encounter. And that doctor, too, so bent on his destruction. They are on the terrace now. How beautiful the lawns and shrubberies look, with the level rays of the rising moon making widely latticed patterns of shimmering shadows across the velvet turf. How refreshing to sit here on the rustic seat after the heat of the ballroom and the strain of avoiding an unwelcome proposal.

Then Mabel recollects herself and glances at Charlemagne. The glance is sufficient to warn her of the danger lurking. The solicitor, so used to being before the bar, begins clearing his throat in a nervous way. He is partly smitten with Mabel's good looks, but more so with Mr Ellis's oil barrels. All his eloquence must serve him just now. Is she about to fly? She looks quite like an unwilling witness.

'Miss Ellis, pardon me and give me your ear for a moment. I have a case to go before you, er … er … a case of love at first sight. You will give judgement in the case. But your judgement I crave be tempered with mercy for, er, the unlucky man who has staked his all.'

'Pardon me', Mr Riles, I am not competent to give judgement on so serious a case. My experience of the tender passion has been nil, I assure you. Besides, see the day breaking yonder. Some of our guests will be wanting to depart and I should be there to see them out. Allow me to withhold judgement for another occasion.'

'Pardon me for detaining you, Miss Mabel, but I assure you I had not noticed the breaking day, by other signs do I measure day. It is day when you are near. Elsewhere the blackness of Hades surrounds me.'

'Now Mr Riles, of all people living, I never credited *you* with having a desire to pay empty compliments. Do allow me to go. See the sun is rising. What will uncle say?'

'Uncle, uncle, it is always uncle. Would it not be wiser to adopt a more dear and loving title?' He seizes her hands to prevent her escape. 'I have long awaited an opportune moment to unburden myself of a load of heaped-up − yes I may say heaped-up − for even before the Woolsack I am so far forgetful of my position and mindful of you as to pile high in my mind terms of ...'

'Faith, it is all about all you are capable of, piling up your terms, you close-fisted old parchment, you− let go of the lady you beggarly parvenu.'

'Do you dare to interfere to put me into a furore?'

As the solicitor still holds unwilling Mabel's hand, the doctor catches him by the collar and shakes him, upon which there is an evident intention on the part of both to come to blows. Suddenly from the window bursts forth Brutus.

'Go show your slaves how choleric you are. By the gods you shall digest the venom of your spleen though it do split you'.

With a growl the emperor lets go and turns to Brutus.

'What the hang brought you, you infernal nobody, putting your foot into my affairs? I'll teach you.'

The solicitor adds, 'And may I ask what the hang, in your polite parlance, took you here tonight like a worried hen putting your foot where it wasn't wanted?'

'Good gentlemen, look fresh and merrily. Let not our looks put on our purposes. Perhaps Brutus might be able to help you if you convey your annoyance to him. What has really occurred to put two such excellent gentlemen out of temper?'

'Hang you, no' exclaims the solicitor. 'I must follow Miss Mabel and finish my honourable proposal but the doctor hangs on to her coattails.'

'I tell you; you shall not go. I got the first innings before this hangman came on the scene.'

What a sight it was to look at the fat doctor pulling at the attorney's dress suit, the latter making spasmodic darts for the house and for the dodging doctor in the rear. While Brutus, his arms crossed and his eyes fixed and with the manner of a cattle dealer, exclaims: 'Would he were fatter but I fear him not. Fear him not, Caesar, he is not dangerous.'

Now Mr Ellis, bearing full witness to the commotion between these two gentlemen, obviously had a change of heart as, before bidding farewell to all, he turned to Mabel and gave what could only be interpreted as a wink of approval.

The Swinging of the Bell in Raheenmore

By Nora Feehan

At the dawning of the Sabbath in the year of '33
The snow lay fathoms deep on bush and tree
It rolled like mountain ranges all along the Blackwood Road
And cast its mantle while o'er vale and lea.

And peering thro' his window stood our curate Father Joe
Listening to the blizzard's dismal roar,
He sadly shook his head and sighed "I fear I cannot go
And no bell will ring today in Raheenmore."

"What ho! My Pat in yonder hut, arise and get ye here
The curate waits your services awhile
Alarm town and country, for the Judgment Day is near

Up! Up! And try to get across the stile."

Rush up to Kilavalley, and tear them out of bed

To clear the road before me, from this door,

Get pick and spade and shovel, if you put them where you know

For the bell must ring today in Raheenmore.

"Yes, Father," shouted Paddy, "Sure I'm near across the hedge

And my head is halfway out above the snow

And I'll get the old grey pony if you cannot go yourself,

And we'll head atop the hedge if you must go."

My jewel you are, good Paddy! Up and over quick and soon,

Gather all the men and boys out for the race,

To Alaska we'll be making, put your dolman round your neck;

Get the snow plough into gear at your own pace."

And soon a noble cavalcade, along the three-mile trail

With spade and rake and shovel men before

The boys led the old pony with our curate on his back

And he said the Mass that day in Raheenmore.

And the old bell tinkled, tinkled from its belfry on a tree

And echoed round the hills to Ballingaore,

And a congregation gathered thro' the blizzard and the snow

To hear the holy Mass in Raheenmore.

But soon a grander tone shall float across the fields of spring

And Father James shall read the Mass and the Regina sing

And John of Meath has come afar to start the new bells chime

To echo o'er the forest green to many a far-off time.

And from a far and far-off land will come an ancient race,

With Father Joe to lead the van back to a well-loved place,

To join the worship of the King as oft they come of yore

Through snow and storm to hear the Mass in the church of Raheenmore.

Fairest White Rose of My Heart

By Nora Feehan

(Sent by me on chance to John McCormac, who never acknowledged it but made Song of My Heart his film The Rose of Tralee soon after. Incidentally, it was about a beloved cow that I wrote, not a young lady.)

Down where the murmuring breezes
Whisper old tales to the sedge .
Lies my young love softly dreaming
There by the bright streamlet's edge
Round her my thoughts are entwining
Nor for a moment would stray
She is my Queen of the Morning
She is my dream of the day
CHORUS
She is my fairest, my Rose
She is my queen of the morn
In her all treasures repose
In her soft eyes are reborn
Tenderest thoughts that have been

Tenderest dreams that depart
She is my fairest and she's my queen
the fairest White Rose of my Heart ...

Many a rival I own
There by the murmuring rill
Flowers of summer, soft blooming
Winds, that sing songs on the hill
Bog birds that glide thro' the rain
Winds that sweep in from the sea
Each has a share of her love
Each stands between her and me but ...
CHORUS
She is my fairest, my Rose
She is my dream of the morn
In her all treasures repose
In her soft eyes are reborn
Tenderest thoughts that have been
Tenderest dreams that depart
For she is my fairest
And she is my queen
Fairest White Rose of my Heart

St Brigid on Croghan Hill

By Nora Feehan

On the slopes of Croghan
See the gentle novice
Brigid of the tender heart
Young, fair and free.
Lambkins skip about her feet,
Little birds sing around her,
Cows with soft round eyes draw near
Who so loved as she

Loved by God and loved by man
Loved by every creature,
For her creed is Love alone
Mary of the Gael,
Far and wide she sows her seed
And through grace abounding
In the country of her love
Not one grain shall fail

Brigid may we meet you on the shining hilltops

In the fields of paradise when this life is over

May we be amongst that flock

That you bring from Erin

O'er the restless sea of life

To the golden shore

Reference Sources

A Dictionary of Hiberno-English by Terence Patrick Dolan

Slanlanguage ‒ a dictionary of IRISH Slang by Bernard Share

Appendix

Samples of Nora's notes and art and
photographs from Westmeath 1904,
courtesy of late Dr Edward Tynan
(1868-1940) granduncle of Oliver Daly

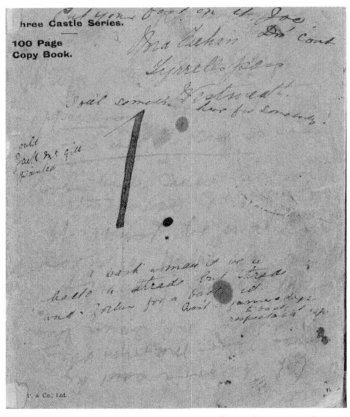

Nora's copy where she wrote her short stories
and poems

Among the Hills of Ardnaree.
(A Tale of Fifty years ago)
(By "Francis O'Fiachran") CHAP 1.

Kind, kind & gentle is she.
Kind is my Mary.
The tender blossom on the tree,
Cannot compare with Mary.

It was a red-letter day in Mary McLaughlin's life, this, and there was joy in her bright young face, and sunshine in the dark brown depths of her eyes, as she tripped along the moss-grown pathway, under the big trees of the wood; for Mary had an inveterate dislike to roads, seeing that they generally led, in the long 'n the short, to towns; but in here, among the giants and the dwarfs, plant life, she was in her glory.

Not a glimpse of the wide highway, with its stifling grey sheton'; winches could wind itself through the crumbling wall, to detract from the primeval loneliness of the scene. And surely since the far-off days, when her ancestors, the great McLaughlins, had caused these grand old beeches and chestnuts to be planted,

Among the Hills of Ardnaree

" When Mollie was in the Ribbonmen "
by Nora ní Fhiacáin.

What was the attraction that drew half the bone
and sinew of the parish to Farrelly's cabin
on winter nights when the summer's saving
would be flaming & roaring and making
war with the bog wind in the big chimney,
or on summer eves when they should be
wielding the caman, or sending the foot-
-ball over the hills for the honour & glory
of the old county? Was it the bits of
information that Willeen was in the habit
of dispensing at the top of his voice from
the "Reporter" as he lay in the open
settlebed after the day's work? or was it a share
in the viands which his sister Mollie
prepared in plenty for his supper, and
to a share of which every comer, rich or
poor, young or old, was welcome?
Or — "likeliest thing" you will say - was it for

When Molly was in the Ribbonmen

The Children's Bag.

"Glasson village"

"Ballykurkey. Bridge" "Inny"

"The hawthorn bush, with seats beneath the shade,
For talking age and whispering lovers made!"

Cottage – Kilkenny – West

"Stand" Horse Show Mullingar '04

"the decent church that topp'd the neighbouring hill"
(site of)

"a breakdown on the road to Auburn"

Printed in Great Britain
by Amazon

71231678R00092